Anonymous

National Worthies

Anonymous

National Worthies

ISBN/EAN: 9783337384074

Printed in Europe, USA, Canada, Australia, Japan

Cover: Foto ©ninafisch / pixelio.de

More available books at **www.hansebooks.com**

NATIONAL WORTHIES
BEING·A·SELECTION· FROM·THE·NATIONAL· PORTRAIT·GALLERY·

WESTMINSTER·
ARCHIBALD
CONSTABLE·AND·
COMPANY·····
MDCCCXCIX·

The thanks of the Publishers are due to the Director of the National Portrait Gallery, and also to Mr. G. F. Watts, R.A., for permission to reproduce the portraits in this volume.

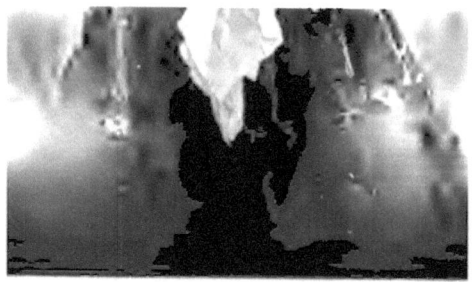

PLATE I.   HER MAJESTY, QUEEN VICTORIA.

PLATE II.
RIGHT HON. WILLIAM EWART GLADSTONE, P.C., LL.D., D.C.L., F.R.S.

PLATE III. CARDINAL HENRY EDWARD MANNING, D.D.

PLATE IV.   PROFESSOR SIR RICHARD OWEN, K.C.B., M.D., F.R.S.

PLATE V.   ALFRED, FIRST BARON TENNYSON.

PLATE VI.   CARDINAL JOHN HENRY NEWMAN, D.D.

PLATE VII.   WILLIAM WILKIE COLLINS.

PLATE VIII.   ROBERT BROWNING.

PLATE IX.   MATTHEW ARNOLD.

PLATE X. RIGHT HON. ANTHONY ASHLEY-COOPER,
Seventh Earl of Shaftsbury, K.G., D.C.L.

PLATE XI.   CHARLES ROBERT DARWIN, LL.D., F.R.S.

PLATE XII.   THOMAS CARLYLE.

PLATE XIII. SIR ROWLAND HILL, K.C.B.

PLATE XIV.
JOHN LAIRD MAIR, LORD LAWRENCE, G.C.B., K.C.S.I., D.C.L., LL.D.

PLATE XV.   MISS AGNES STRICKLAND.

PLATE XVI.   SIR EDWIN HENRY LANDSEER, R.A.

PLATE XVII.   DAVID LIVINGSTONE, LL.D., D.C.L.

PLATE XIX. ELIZABETH O'NEILL.

PLATE XX. CHARLES DICKENS.

Plate XXI.   Samuel Lover.

PLATE XXII.   MICHAEL FARADAY.

PLATE XXIII.   RICHARD COBDEN, M.P.

PLATE XXIV.   WALTER SAVAGE LANDOR.

PLATE XXV.   JOHN LEECH.

PLATE XXVI.   GENERAL SIR JAMES OUTRAM, BART., G.C.B.

Plate XXVII.   William Makepeace Thackeray.

PLATE XXVIII.　　ELIZABETH BARRETT BROWNING.

Plate XXIX.   H.R.H. Albert, Prince Consort of England.

PLATE XXX.
RIGHT HON. THOMAS BABINGTON, M.P., LORD MACAULAY.

PLATE XXXI.   JAMES HENRY LEIGH HUNT.

PLATE XXXII.   THOMAS DE QUINCEY.

Plate XXXIII.   Admiral Sir John Ross, C.B.

PLATE XXXIV. SIR HENRY ROWLEY BISHOP.

Plate XXXV. Sir William Edward Parry, F.R.S.

PLATE XXXVI.   ARTHUR WELLESLEY, DUKE OF WELLINGTON.

PLATE XXXVII.   WILLIAM WORDSWORTH.

PLATE XXXVIII. SIR MARC ISAMBARD BRUNEL.

PLATE XXXIX.   GEORGE STEPHENSON.

PLATE XL. REAR-ADMIRAL SIR JOHN FRANKLIN.

PLATE XLII. THOMAS HOOD.

PLATE XLIII.   ROBERT SOUTHEY, LL.D.

Plate XLIV.   Thomas Arnold, D.D.

Plate XLV.   Grace Horsley Darling.

PLATE XLVI.   THEODORE EDWARD HOOK.

PLATE XLVII.   SIR DAVID WILKIE, R.A.

PLATE XLVIII.   JOHN CONSTABLE, R.A.

Plate XLIX.   Joseph Grimaldi.

Plate L.   Rev. Edward Irving, M.A.

Plate LI. Charles Lamb.

PLATE LII. JOHN O'KEEFFE.

PLATE LIII.　WILLIAM WILBERFORCE, M.P.

PLATE LIV.   SIR WALTER SCOTT, BART.

PLATE LV.   PATRICK NASMYTH.

PLATE LVI.   SARAH SIDDONS.

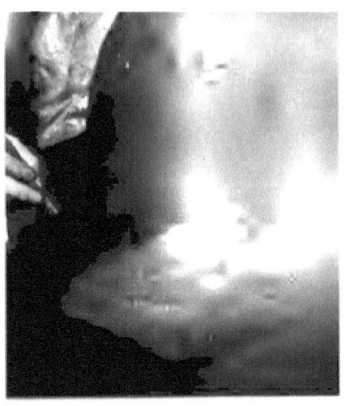

PLATE LVII.   WILLIAM BLAKE.

PLATE LVIII. REV. SAMUEL PARR, LL.D.

PLATE LIX.   GEORGE GORDON (Sixth LORD BYRON).

PLATE LX.   DR. EDWARD JENNER, F.R.S.

PLATE LXI. SIR WILLIAM HERSCHEL, F.R.S.

PLATE LXII.   JAMES WATT.

PLATE LXIII.   RIGHT HON. WARREN HASTINGS.

PLATE LXIV.   MATTHEW GREGORY LEWIS, M.P.

PLATE LXV.   JOHN PHILPOT CURRAN.

PLATE LXVI. RIGHT HON. RICHARD BRINSLEY SHERIDAN, M.P.

Plate LXVII.   Emma, Lady Hamilton.

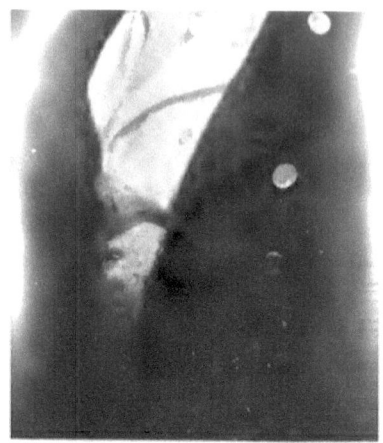

PLATE LXVIII. CHARLES DIBDIN.

Right Hon. Chas. James Fox, M.P.

PLATE LXX.   HORATIO, VISCOUNT NELSON.

PLATE LXXI.   HORATIO, VISCOUNT NELSON

PLATE LXXII.   GEORGE ROMNEY.

PLATE LXXIII. GEORGE WASHINGTON.

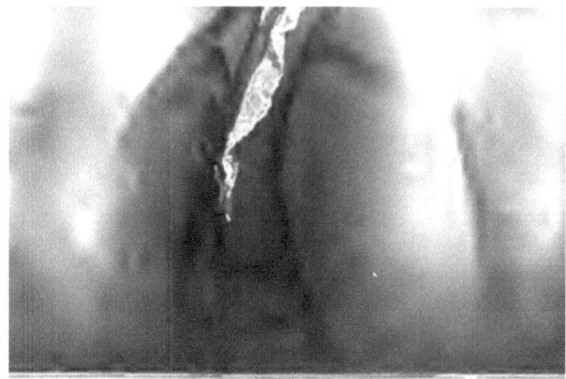

PLATE LXXIV.   RIGHT HON. EDMUND BURKE, M.P.

PLATE LXXV.   HORACE WALPOLE.

PLATE LXXVI.   ROBERT BURNS.

PLATE LXXVII.   JOHN HUNTER.

PLATE LXXVIII. SIR JOSHUA REYNOLDS, P.R.A.

PLATE LXXIX.   JOHN SMEATON, F.R.S.

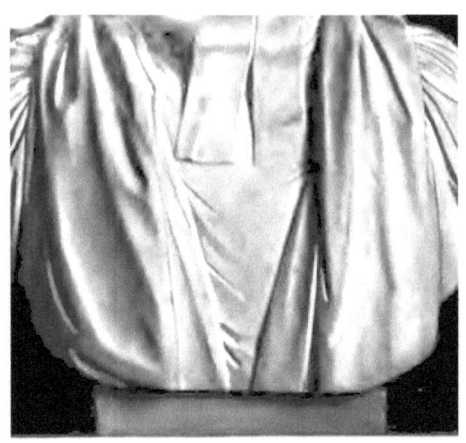

PLATE LXXX. REV JOHN WESLEY, M.A.

PLATE LXXXI.   BENJAMIN FRANKLIN.

PLATE LXXXII.   JOHN HOWARD.

PLATE LXXXIII. PRINCE CHARLES EDWARD STUART.

PLATE LXXXIV.   THOMAS GAINSBOROUGH, R.A.

PLATE LXXXV. AUGUSTUS, VISCOUNT KEPPEL.

PLATE LXXXVI.   SIR WILLIAM BLACKSTONE.

PLATE LXXXVII.   CAPTAIN JAMES COOK, R.N.

PLATE LXXXVIII. DAVID GARRICK.

1

PLATE XC.   WILLIAM PITT, FIRST EARL OF CHATHAM.

PLATE XCI.   WILLIAM HOGARTH.

PLATE XCII. SAMUEL RICHARDSON.

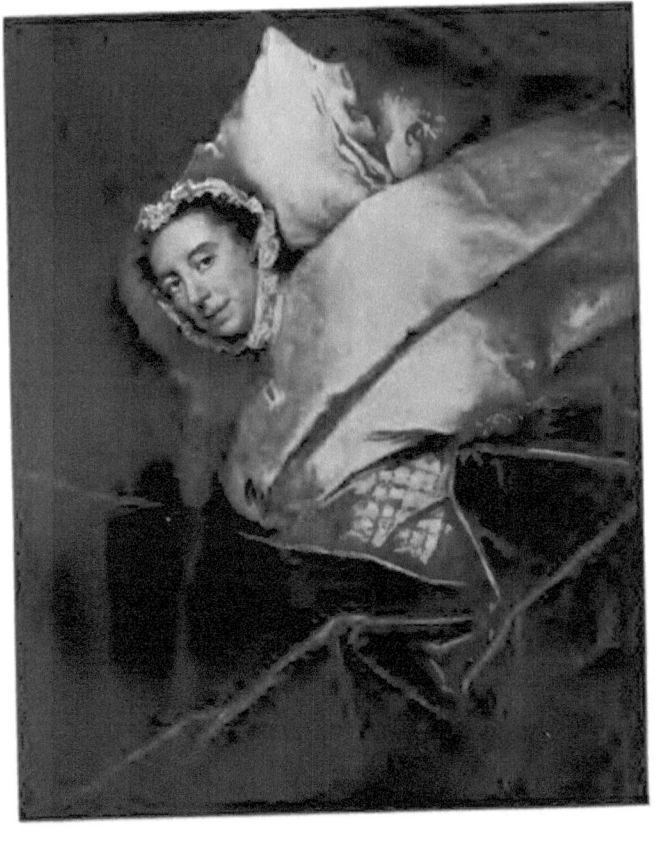

Plate XCIII. Margaret Woffington.

Plate XCIV.   George Frederick Handel.

PLATE XCV.   GENERAL JAMES WOLFE.

PLATE XCVI.   REV. ISAAC WATTS, D.D.

PLATE XCVII.   JONATHAN SWIFT, D.D.

PLATE XCVIII. ALEXANDER POPE.

PLATE XCIX.   HON. ROGER NORTH.

PLATE CI.   SIR ISAAC NEWTON, F.R.S.

PLATE CIII.   RIGHT HON. JOSEPH ADDISON.

PLATE CIV.   GILBERT BURNET, D.D.

PLATE CV.   THOMAS BETTERTON.

PLATE CVI.   BARBARA VILLIERS, DUCHESS OF CLEVELAND.

CVII.   CATHERINE OF BRAGANZA.

PLATE CVIII. TITUS OATES.

Plate CIX. John Locke.

PLATE CX.   SAMUEL PEPYS, P.R.S.

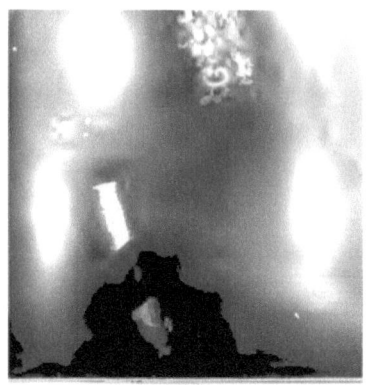

Plate CXL.   King William III.

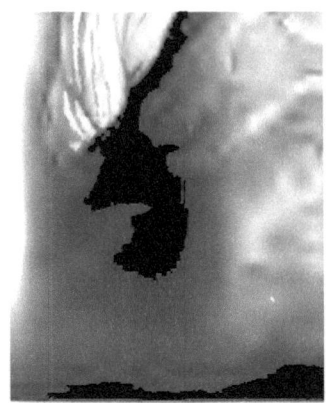

Plate CXII. John Dryden.

PLATE CXIII. THE SEVEN BISHOPS.

PLATE CXIV.   ELEANOR GWYNN.

PLATE CXV. JAMES SCOTT, DUKE OF MONMOUTH, K.G.

PLATE CXVI. CHARLES II.

PLATE CXVII.   PRINCE RUPERT, K.G.

PLATE CXVIII. SAMUEL BUTLER.

PLATE CXIX.   MARY DAVIS.

PLATE CXX.   ANDREW MARVEL.

PLATE CXXI. EDWARD COCKER.

PLATE CXXII.   EDWARD HYDE, FIRST EARL OF CLARENDON.

PLATE CXXIII.   JOHN MILTON.

Plate CXXIV.   Queen Henrietta Maria.

PLATE CXXV. WILLIAM HARVEY, M.D.

PLATE CXXVI.   INIGO JONES.

PLATE CXXVII.   HENRY IRETON.

PLATE CXXVIII.   KING CHARLES I.

PLATE CXXIX.   WILLIAM LAUD.

PLATE CXXXI.   SIR JOHN SUCKLING.

PLATE CXXXII.   BEN JONSON.

PLATE CXXXIII.
CHILDREN OF KING CHARLES I., WITH A LARGE DOG.

Plate CXXXIV.   Francis Bacon.

PLATE CXXXV.   WILLIAM CAMDEN.

PLATE CXXXVI.   SIR WALTER RALLIGH.

Plate CXXXVII.   William Shakspeare.

PLATE CXXXVIII.

THE GUNPOWDER PLOT CONSPIRATORS, viz., GUY FAWKES, ROBERT CATESBY, THOMAS PERCY, JOHN WRIGHT, CHRISTOPHER WRIGHT, ROBERT WINTER, THOMAS WINTER AND THOMAS BATES.

PLATE CXXXIX.   QUEEN ELIZABETH.

PLATE CXL. WILLIAM CECIL, LORD BURGHLEY, K.G.

PLATE CXLI.   MARY, QUEEN OF SCOTS.

PLATE CXLIII.   JOHN KNOX.

PLATE CXLIV.   HENRY, LORD DARNLEY.

Plate CXLV. Thomas Cranmer, D.D.

PLATE CXLVI.   HUGH LATIMER, D.D.

PLATE CXLVII.   LADY JANE GREY.

PLATE CXLVIII. HENRY VIII.

PLATE CXLIX. ANNE BOLEYN.

PLATE CL. CATHERINE OF ARRAGON.

PLATE CLI. THOMAS WOLSEY.

PLATE CLII.   KING HENRY V.

PLATE CLIII.   GEOFFREY CHAUCER.

PLATE CLIV. EDWARD, THE BLACK PRINCE.

PLATE I.

HER MAJESTY, VICTORIA, by the Grace of God, of the United Kingdom of Great Britain and Ireland, Queen, Defender of the Faith, Empress of India (in India Kaiser-i-Hind), born, 24th May, 1819; succeeded to the Throne, 20th June, 1837, on the death of her uncle, King William IV.; crowned, 28th June, 1838; married, 10th February, 1840, to his late Royal Highness Francis Albert Augustus Charles Emmanuel, Prince Consort. Proclaimed Empress of India, 1st January, 1877.

A copy in water colours by Julia J. G. Lady Abercromby, after the original portrait by Professor H. Von Angeli, taken in 1875.

PLATE II.

RIGHT HON. WILLIAM EWART GLADSTONE, P.C., LL.D., D.C.L., F.R.S., Statesman and Essayist. Fourth son of Sir John Gladstone, merchant. Born at Liverpool, 1809. Educated at Eton and Christ Church, Oxford. Married Catherine, daughter of Sir Stephen Glynne, of Hawarden Castle, 1839. M.P. for Newark, 1832-37; M.P. for Oxford University, 1846. Lord Rector of Edinburgh University, 1859-65. Chancellor of the Exchequer, 1852-55; 1859-66; 1868-74; 1880-82. Premier, 1868; 1880-85; 1886; 1892-94. Began Midlothian Campaign, 1879. Romanes Lecturer at Oxford, 1892. Retired from political life, 1895. Died at Hawarden, 1898, and buried in Westminster Abbey. Painted by G. F. Watts, R.A., in 1865.

Plate III.

HENRY EDWARD MANNING, D.D., Cardinal Archbishop of Westminster. Youngest son of William Manning, a West India merchant. Born, 1808, at Copped Hall, Totteridge, Herts. Educated at Harrow and Balliol College, Oxford. Made Fellow of Merton, 1832. Married Miss Sargent, sister-in-law of Bishop Wilberforce. Rector of Wool-lavington and Graffham, Sussex, 1833. Archdeacon of Chichester, 1840 to 1851. Joined the Church of Rome, 1851. Succeeded Cardinal Wiseman as Archbishop of Westminster, 1865. Made Cardinal, 1875. Besides numerous volumes of sermons he wrote " The Temporal Power of the Pope " and " The True Story of the Vatican Council." The Cardinal was an earnest supporter of the temperance movement. Died, 1892, in London, and buried at St. Mary's Cemetery, Kensal Green.

"He was almost great from the insight with which he recognised, and the energy with which he strove to put into effect the power which might come to the Roman Catholic Church from a union with the democracy."

Painted by G. F. Watts, R.A., in 1882, and presented by the artist.

Plate IV.

PROFESSOR SIR RICHARD OWEN, K.C.B., M.D., F.R.S., Naturalist and eminent authority on comparative anatomy and osteology, especially of extinct species. Younger son of Richard Owen, a West India merchant. Born at Lancaster, 1804. Educated at Lancaster Grammar School, and Edinburgh University, and Paris. Became a lecturer at St. Bartholomew's Hospital, 1829. Conservator of the Hunterian Museum of the Royal College of Surgeons, and Superintendent, 1856, of the Natural History Departments in the British Museum. Was created C.B. in 1873. Died 1892 at Sheen Lodge and buried at Ham, near Richmond.

" From the examination in 1839 of a fossil bone sent to him from New Zealand he propounded a theory of the existence in remote ages of a gigantic bird, the accuracy of his theory being established by the latter discovery of the whole fossil. This led him to the adoption of his famous theory of the extinction of species."

Painted by H. W. Pickersgill, R.A., in 1845.

PLATE V.

ALFRED, FIRST BARON TENNYSON, Poet Laureate. The fourth of twelve children of Rev. W. G. C. Tennyson. Born at Somersby Rectory, in Lincolnshire, 1809. Educated at Louth Grammar School and Trinity College, Cambridge, 1828. Gained the Chancellor's Medal for "Timbuctoo," 1829. Married Emily, daughter of Henry Sellwood, and appointed Poet Laureate, 1850. First published in 1827, in association with his brother Charles, " Poems by Two Brothers "; " Poems," 1832; " The Princess," 1847; "In Memoriam," 1850; " Maud and other Poems," 1855; " Idylls of the King," 1859; " Enoch Arden," 1864; " The Holy Grail and other Poems," 1869; "Gareth and Lynette and other Poems," 1872 ; "Queen Mary," 1875 ; "Harold," 1876; "The Lovers' Tale," 1879 ; " The Cup," 1881 ; " Becket," 1884 ; " Locksley Hall, sixty years after," and "The Promise of May," 1886; " Demeter and other Poems," 1889. Created a peer, 1884. Died 1892, and buried in Westminster Abbey.

"Tennyson is endowed precisely in points where Wordsworth wanted! There is no finer ear, nor more command of the keys of lauguage. Colour like the dawn flows over the horizon from his pencil, in waves so rich that we do not miss the central form."

Painted by G. F. Watts, R.A., in 1865, and presented by the artist.

PLATE VI.

CARDINAL JOHN HENRY NEWMAN, D.D., Divine, Poet and Writer. Eldest child of John Newman, banker. Born in London, 1801. Educated at the School of Dr. Nicholas, at Ealing, whence he passed in 1816 to Trinity College, Oxford ; elected Fellow of Oriel College, 1822, and Incumbent of St. Mary's, Oxford, 1828. Deprived of his tutorship, 1832. One of the principal leaders of what is known as "the Oxford movement." Joined the Church of Rome, 1845. Founded the London Oratory and that of St. Philip Neri, in Birmingham, 1850. Elected Honorary Fellow of Trinity College, Oxford, 1877, and created a Cardinal in 1879. A vindication of his position was published under the title of "Apologia pro vitâ suâ." As author of the hymn " Lead, Kindly Light," which " belonged to the Church Universal " he obtained world-wide fame. Died 1890, and buried at Rednall.

" One of the masters of English prose, as well as a potent force in the religious movement of the age."

Painted in 1889 by Miss Emmeline Deane, and presented by Dr. G. Vernon Blunt.

PLATE. VII.

WILLIAM WILKIE COLLINS, Novelist, eldest son of William Collins, R.A. Born in London, 1824. Educated at Highbury. Author of "After Dark," 1856; "The Dead Secret," 1857; "The Woman in White," 1860; "No Name," 1862; "Armadale," 1866; "Moonstone," 1868; "The New Magdalen," 1873; and two plays, "The Lighthouse" and "The Frozen Deep." Famous for the elaboration and sensational character of his plots. Died in London, September, 1889, and buried at Kensal Green.

"For ingenuity, for cleverness, for power of raising curiosity and keeping interest alive, Mr. Collins stands altogether alone. The art is not a high art, perhaps; but he has mastered it, and mastered it—as his books show—by honest industry.

Painted by Sir J. E. Millais, P.R.A.

PLATE VIII.

ROBERT BROWNING, Poet. Born at Camberwell, 1812. Son of "a clerk, highly placed in the house of Rothschild." Educated at a private school in Peckham, at University College, London, and abroad. Published "Pauline," in 1833; "Paracelsus," in 1835; "Strafford,"—his first drama—in 1837; "Bells and Pomegranates," 1841-46; "Men and Women," 1855; "Dramatis Personæ," 1864; "The Ring and the Book," 1867; "Balaustion's Adventure," 1871; "Fifine at the Fair," 1872; "The Agamemnon," 1877; "Dramatic Idylls," 1879 and 1880; and his last volume "Asolando" was published on the day of his death. Married Elizabeth Barrett, the poetess, 1846. Died in Venice, December 12th, 1889. Buried in Westminster Abbey.

"No poet since Burns—none, perhaps, since Shakespeare—has known and felt so deeply as Mr. Browning the pathos of human life."

Painted by G. F. Watts, R.A., in 1875, and presented by the artist.

PLATE IX.

MATTHEW ARNOLD, Poet, Critic and Essayist. Born at Laleham, Middlesex, 1822. Eldest son of Dr. Thomas Arnold, Head Master of Rugby School. Educated at Winchester, Rugby, and Oxford. Elected Fellow of Oriel, 1845, an Inspector of Schools, 1851, and Professor of Poetry at Oxford, 1857. Best known for his Newdigate prize poem on "Cromwell," 1843, for his volume "The Schools and Universities of the Continent," 1868; "Essays in Criticism," 1865, and "Literature and Dogma," 1873. Other notable volumes are "The Strayed Reveller and other Poems," 1849; "Empedocles and other Poems," 1853; "Merope," 1857; "Culture and Anarchy," 1869; "Poetical Works," 1869; "God and the Bible," 1875; "Essays in Criticism," 2nd series, 1888. He died suddenly at Liverpool, 1888, and was buried at Laleham.

"He is an academical poet, reflecting the mental attitude of the most cultured minds of his time, and also their obligations to antiquity and such moderns as Wordsworth and Goethe."

Painted by G. F. Watts, R.A., in 1881, and presented by the artist.

PLATE X.

RIGHT HON. ANTHONY ASHLEY-COOPER, Seventh Earl of Shaftesbury, K.G., D.C.L., Philanthropist and Politician. Born in London, 1801. Educated at Harrow and Christ Church, Oxford. First entered Parliament as Lord Ashley, M.P. for Woodstock, in 1826. He devoted his life to the reform of the factory system, and was largely instrumental in securing the passing of the Ten Hours Bill in 1847, and the exclusion of female labour and of boys under 13 years of age from mines. He was mainly the promoter and the first President of the Ragged School Union. Married Lady Emily Cooper, 1830. Succeeded to the Earldom in 1851. Died at Folkestone, 1885.

"There never existed a man of more benevolence, more worth, and true piety." This remark, made by Bishop Huntingford of the fourth is equally applicable to the seventh earl.

Painted by G. F. Watts, R.A., and presented by the artist.

PLATE XI.

CHARLES ROBERT DARWIN, LL.D., F.R.S., Naturalist and Scientist. Son of Robert Waring Darwin, grandson of Dr. Erasmus Darwin, and (on his mother's side) of Josiah Wedgwood. Born at Shrewsbury in 1809. Educated at Shrewsbury School, at Edinburgh University, and Christ's College, Cambridge, 1828. Most famous for "On the Origin of Species by means of Natural Selection," published in 1859, and for "The Descent of Man and Selection in Relation to Sex," published in 1871. He was naturalist on board the "Beagle" during its expedition to complete the Survey of Patagonia, S. America, and the Pacific, 1831-36. Married Emma Wedgwood, 1839. Died at Down, in Kent, 1882, and buried in Westminster Abbey.

"The most potent instrument for the extension of the realm of natural knowledge which has come into men's hands since the publication of Newton's "Principia" is Darwin's "Origin of Species."

Painted by the Hon. John Collier, being a replica, with certain alterations, of the portrait painted for the Linnean Society in 1881.

PLATE XII.

THOMAS CARLYLE, Historian and Essayist. Born at Ecclefechan, Dumfrieshire, in 1795. Son of a stonemason. Educated at Annan Academy and Edinburgh University. Began life as a schoolmaster at Annan and Kirkcaldy. Married in 1826, Jane, daughter of Dr. John Welsh. Published "Life of Schiller," 1823-4. Contributed "Sartor Resartus" to "Fraser's Magazine," 1833-4. Came to Chelsea in 1834. "The French Revolution" appeared in 1837; "Oliver Cromwell's Letters and Speeches" ten years later, and "The History of Frederick the Second, called Frederick the Great," from 1858 to 1865. The first collected edition of Carlyle's works was published 1857 to 1858. Died at Chelsea in 1881, and buried at Ecclefechan.

"As a representative author, a literary figure, no man else will bequeath to the future more significant hints of our stormy era, its fierce paradoxes, its din and its struggling parturition periods, than Carlyle."

Painted in 1869, by G. F. Watts, R.A., and presented by the artist.

PLATE XIII.

SIR ROWLAND HILL, K.C.B., Founder of the Uniform Penny Post. Third Son of Thomas Wright Hill. Born at Kidderminster in 1795. Commenced life as a schoolmaster, and published, early in 1837, " Post Office Reform, its Importance and Practicability," and succeeded in introducing his scheme for a uniform and low postage with stamps for prepayment, in 1840. Was appointed permanent Secretary to the Postmaster General in 1846, and succeeded Colonel Maberley as Chief Secretary in 1854. As a Director of the Brighton Railway established the system of express trains and cheap Sunday tickets. He retired in 1864, and died at Hampstead, in 1879. Buried in Westminster Abbey.

" It will be the glory of England for all time that she was the first country to adopt this ray of light."

Painted by J. A. Vinter.

PLATE XIV.

JOHN LAIRD MAIR, LORD LAWRENCE, G.C.B. K.C.S.I., D.C.L., LL.D., Governor General of India. Sixth son of Lieut.-Colonel Alexander Lawrence. Born at Richmond, Yorkshire, in 1811. Educated at College Green, Bristol, Foyle College, Londonderry, and at Haileybury. Went to India in 1829 and became commissioner of the provinces added to the Indian Empire after the first Sikh War; was appointed Chief Commissioner of the Punjaub when that province was annexed in 1849. Distinguished himself during the great Mutiny of 1857, and succeeded Lord Elgin as Viceroy of India, in 1863. Was raised to the peerage on his retirement in 1869. Was chairman of the London School Board from 1870 to 1873. Married Harriete Catherine Hamilton, 1841. Died in London, 1879, and buried in Westminster Abbey.

" Lord Lawrence was a servant of the Indian Government who left his mark upon the history of the Empire. He reorganised the Punjaub under British rule, and kept the province true to England during the Mutiny. He was one of the most zealous and laborious of viceroys."

Painted by G. F. Watts, R.A., on Lord Lawrence's return from India, and presented by the artist.

PLATE XV.

AGNES STRICKLAND, Authoress. Born in London, 1796, Second surviving daughter of Thomas Strickland, of Reydon Hall, Suffolk. Famous for her " Lives of the Queens of England " and "Scotland," 1840-8, and 1850-59. Died at Southwold, 1874, and buried there.

"Miss Strickland's interesting volumes are particularly valuable to the historian for the copious extracts which they contain from curious unpublished documents which had escaped the notice of writers too exclusively occupied with political events to give much heed to details of a domestic and personal character."

Painted in 1846 by J. Hayes.

PLATE XVI.

SIR EDWIN HENRY LANDSEER, R.A., Animal Painter. Born in London, 1802. Third son of John Landseer, A.E.R.A., the engraver. Studied art under his father, at the R.A., and under B. R. Haydon. Exhibited at the Royal Academy for the first time in 1817. Elected an Associate, 1826, and a full Academician in 1831. He was knighted in 1850. Refused the office of P.R.A. upon the death of Sir Charles Eastlake, in 1865. He died at St. John's Wood, 1873, and was buried in St. Paul's Cathedral.

"Down to about 1823 he was content to represent the natural expression and character of animals; after that date his animal pieces are generally made subservient to some sentiment or idea."

Painted in 1855, by Sir Francis Grant, P.R.A.

PLATE XVII.

DAVID LIVINGSTONE, LL.D., D.C.L., Missionary and Explorer. Second son of Neil Livingstone. Born at Blantyre, near Glasgow, in 1813. Was sent out to Port Natal by the London Missionary Society in 1840. He married Mary, daughter of Rev. Robert Moffat, in 1844, and devoted his life to missionary work and the exploration of the interior of Africa. Expeditions were sent out in search of him in 1867 and 1870. His best known writings were "Travels and Researches in South Africa," 1857, "Expeditions to the Zambesi," 1865, and "Last Journals." He died of dysentery at Ilala, near Lake Bangweolo, in 1873, and was buried in Westminster Abbey.

"His extensive travels place him at the head of modern explorers, for no one has dared as yet to penetrate where he has been; no one through a lengthy series of years has devoted so much of his life to the work of searching out tribes hitherto unknown."

Painted by Frederick Havill.

PLATE XVIII.

JOHN STUART MILL, M.P. Political Economist, Philosopher, and Essayist. Born in London, 1806, eldest son of James Mill, the historian of British India. Entirely and severely educated by his father. Entered the India House as a clerk in 1823, and remained until the transfer of the India Government to the Crown, 1858. Published "A System of Logic," 1843, "Principles of Political Economy," 1848, "On Liberty," 1859, "Representative Government," 1861, and "Utilitarianism," 1863. In 1865 was returned as Liberal M.P. for Westminster. Married Mrs. Taylor, 1851. Died at Avignon in 1873.

"In the vigour and penetration of his intellect he has had few superiors in the history of thought; in the wide compass of the human interests which he served, he was almost equally remarkable; and the energy and determination of his character, giving effect to as single-minded an ardour for the improvement of mankind and of human life as probably ever existed, make his life a memorable example."

Painted by G. F. Watts, R.A., and presented by the artist.

PLATE XIX.

ELIZA O'NEILL, afterwards Lady Belcher, Tragic Actress. Born in Ireland of theatrical parents in 1791. Miss O'Neill played with great success in Dublin and made her début at Covent Garden in "Belvidera," October 13th, 1814, as Juliet, to the Romeo of

Conway. She was most successful, but after a theatrical career of five years retired from the stage and married Mr. W. Wrixon Belcher, M.P., who was created a baronet in 1831. She died in 1872.

"Her excellence—unrivalled by any actress since Mrs. Siddons—consisted in truth of nature and force of passion."

Painted by John J. Masquerier in 1815.

PLATE XX.

CHARLES DICKENS, Novelist. Born at Landport, in Portsea, February 7th, 1812. Son of John Dickens, a clerk in the Navy Pay Office, and Elizabeth Barrow. Entered in the baptismal register as "Charles John Huffham." Educated privately at Chatham and in the Hampstead Road, London. Married Miss Hogarth, 1836. Was placed in a blacking factory at the age of ten, and after leaving school entered a solicitor's office. Became a reporter at Doctors' Commons in his seventeenth year. In 1833 his first original paper, "A Dinner at Poplar Walk," was published. "Sketches by Boz" were collected and published in 1836, and the first number of the "Pickwick Papers" the same year. His other important works are "Oliver Twist," 1838; "Nicholas Nickleby," 1839; "The Old Curiosity Shop," 1840-41; "Barnaby Rudge," 1841; "American Notes," 1842; "Martin Chuzzlewit," 1843; "The Christmas Tales," 1843-46-48; "Dombey & Son," 1846-48; "David Copperfield," 1849-50; "Bleak House," 1852-53; "Little Dorrit," 1855-57; "A Tale of Two Cities," 1859; "Our Mutual Friend," 1864-65; "The Mystery of Edwin Drood" (unfinished). Died at Gadshill, 1870, and buried in Westminster Abbey.

"It is in description that Dickens proved himself so great a master. He laid his hand by instinct upon the salient and characteristic features, and he never failed in finding the right —the only—words fit for their illustration."

"There is no misanthropy in his satire, and no coarseness in his descriptions—a merit enhanced by the nature of his subjects."

Painted by Ary Scheffer in 1856.

PLATE XXI.

SAMUEL LOVER, Novelist, Painter, Musician. Born in Dublin, 1797. Weakness of sight compelled him to abandon the art of miniature painting in 1844. Two years previously he had published "Handy Andy." In 1846 he began to give his "Irish Evenings." He wrote lyric songs, some of which are still popular. He was twice married; died in 1868, at St. Heliers, and was buried at Kensal Green.

"Power may diminish with diversity, but it is a phenomenon after all, that only divides in its particulars to reunite in the sum. Such was the case with Lover."

A marble bust sculptured in 1839 by E. A. Foley.

PLATE XXII.

MICHAEL FARADAY, Electrician, Experimental Chemist and Natural Philosopher. Born at Newington Butts, 1791; the son of a smith. Began life as an errand boy. Attended the lectures of Sir Humphry Davy at the Royal Institution, and in 1813 was appointed his chemical assistant. Married Miss Sarah Barnard, 1821. Appointed Fullerian Professor of Chemistry in 1838, and became famous for his discoveries in connection with electricity and magnetism. He died at Hampton Court in 1867, and was buried in Highgate Cemetery.

"A favourite experiment of his own was representative of himself. He loved to show that water in crystallizing excluded all foreign ingredients, however intimately they might be mixed with it. Out of acids, alkalis, or saline solutions the crystals came sweet and pure. By some such natural process in the formation of this man, beauty and nobleness coalesced to the exclusion of everything vulgar and low."

Painted by Thomas Phillips, R.A., in 1842.

PLATE XXIII.

RICHARD COBDEN, M.P., Corn Law Reformer. Son of William Cobden, a small farmer. Born at Heyshott, near Midhurst, in Sussex, in 1804. Started as calico printer, 1831. Settled in Manchester, 1832. Defeated as parliamentary candidate, 1837, but elected for Southport, 1841; West Riding of Yorkshire, 1847; afterwards for Rochdale. Took a foremost part in securing the repeal of the Corn Duty, 1846, and in popularizing Free Trade.

Successfully negotiated a Commercial Treaty with France. Died in London, 1865, and was buried at Lavington, Sussex.

"The sincerity of his interest in great causes raised him above personalities, as it enabled him to bear with a singular constancy the embarrassments and trials of a life which in some respects had less than its share of happy fortune."

Painted by Lowes Dickinson and presented by members of the Reform Club.

PLATE XXIV.

WALTER SAVAGE LANDOR, poet. Eldest son of Dr. Walter Landor. Born at Ipsley Court, Warwick, 1775. Educated at Rugby and Trinity College, Oxford. Sold his estates and went to the wars (1808), fighting as a volunteer in the Peninsular War. Married Miss Thuillier, 1811. Retired to Italy in 1815 and died in Florence in 1864. His best known works are "Poems," 1795; "Gebir," 1798; "Count Julian," 1812; the "Imaginary Conversations," 1824-29; "Examination of Shakespeare," 1834; "Pericles and Aspasia," 1836; "The Pentameron," 1837; "Hellenics," 1847; "Poemata et Irespictiones," 1847; "Heroic Idylls," 1863.

"By his singularly imposing personal appearance, his imperious will, and his massive intelligence, this 'unsubduable old Roman,' as Carlyle called him, was one of the most original figures among his contemporaries."

Painted by William Fisher.

PLATE XXV.

JOHN LEECH, a famous "Punch" artist. Born in London, 1817, of Irish extraction. Educated at the Charterhouse with Thackeray. Was first "published" in 1840, and a year later joined the ranks of "Punch" artists. To the rare gift of caricature he added great artistic ability and a certain delicacy and refinement too often absent from the works of caricaturists. Married Miss Ann Eaton. He died in 1864, at Kensington, and was buried at Kensal Green.

"He told his story in his drawings more completely than any man of his day; he appealed to every class of society, and touched them all with equal facility, with equal good humour, brightness and beauty."

A water-colour drawing by Sir J. E. Millais, P.R.A., painted in 1854.

PLATE XXVI.

GENERAL SIR JAMES OUTRAM, BART., G.C.B., soldier and administrator. Second son of Benjamin Outram. Born at Butterly Hall, Derbyshire, in 1803. Educated at Udny, Aberdeenshire, and Marischal College, Aberdeen. Sailed for India, 1819, and gazetted lieutenant. Was Chief Commissioner of Oude, in 1856, and succeeded Sir Henry Lawrence as Resident at Lucknow during the Mutiny. He returned to England in 1859; died at Paris, 1863, and was buried in Westminster Abbey.

"The Bayard of India."

"A fox is a fool and a lion a coward compared with James Outram."

Painted by Thomas Brigstocke.

PLATE XXVII.

WILLIAM MAKEPEACE THACKERAY, Novelist. Grandson of Rev. Richard Thackeray, and only child of Richmond Thackeray. Born at Calcutta in 1811. Sent to England, 1817. Educated at the Charterhouse, 1822 to 1828, and Trinity College, Cambridge, 1829-30. Studied art at Rome and on the Continent. Married Isabella Shawe, 1836. Was called to the bar, 1848. Contributed as "Michael Angelo Titmarsh" to "Fraser's Magazine," 1837-38. ("Barry Lyndon" belongs to this period), and published his "Paris Sketch Book," 1840; "Irish Sketch Book," 1843; "Vanity Fair," 1847; "Pendennis," 1849-50; "Esmond," 1852; "The Newcomes," 1854-55; "The Rose and the Ring," 1855; "The Virginians," 1858-59. Edited the "Cornhill Magazine" 1860-62. Left "Denis Duval" uncompleted at his death. Stood for the city of Oxford as a radical, 1857, but was defeated. Died at Kensington, 1863, and was buried at Kensal Green.

"He is, we should say, one of the healthiest writers who has attained celebrity since Scott and Byron. Agreeable, manly, colloquial English—the English of cultivated men, but still with as little bookishness about it as possible—such is the clear atmosphere we breathe in reading him."

Drawn by Samuel Lawrence in 1855.

PLATE XXVIII.

ELIZABETH BARRETT BROWNING, Poetess. Born at Burn Hall, Durham, 1809. Eldest daughter of Edward Moulton, who afterwards took the name of Barrett. At the age of 17 she published "An Essay on Mind"; "Prometheus Bound," 1833; "The Seraphim and other Poems," 1838; "A Drama of Exiles," "A Vision of Poets and the Dead Pan," 1844; "Casa Guidi Windows," 1851; "Aurora Leigh," 1857; and "Poems before Congress," 1860. Married Robert Browning, 1846. Died at Florence, 1861.

"Her wing carries her, without faltering at their obscurity, into the cloud and the mist, where not seldom we fail to follow her, but are tempted, while we admire the honesty of her enthusiasm, to believe that she utters what she herself has but dimly perceived."

"In melodiousness and splendour of poetic gift Mrs. Browning stands first among women."

Drawn in chalk at Rome in 1859 by Field Talfourd.

PLATE XXIX.

H.R.H. FRANCIS ALBERT AUGUSTUS CHARLES EMMANUEL, PRINCE CONSORT. Born at Rosenau, near Cologne, 1819. Second son of Ernest, Duke of Saxe-Coburg-Gotha and of Louise, daughter of Augustus, Duke of Saxe-Gotha-Altenburg. Married at St. James's Palace, February 16th, 1839, to his cousin, Queen Victoria. Elected Chancellor of the University of Cambridge, 1847. Promoted "The Great Exhibition," 1851. Was invested with the title of Prince Consort, 1857. Died at Windsor Castle, 1861, and buried at Frogmore.

"Like Tennyson's 'Arthur,' the Prince Consort was a selfless man, and England has come to know and mourn his loss."

Painted by Franz Xaver Winterhalter, being a replica of the last portrait painted from life, now at Buckingham Palace, and presented by Her Majesty the Queen.

PLATE XXX.

RIGHT HON. THOMAS BABINGTON, M.P., LORD MACAULAY, Historian, Essayist, Statesman and Poet. Born at Rothley Temple, Leicestershire, 1800, eldest son of Zachary Macaulay, the philanthropist. Educated privately and at Trinity College, Cambridge, 1818-24, and called to the Bar in 1826. Entered Parliament as member for Calne in 1830. Exchanged Calne for Leeds, 1832. Went to India in 1834 as legal adviser to the Supreme Council of Calcutta, for the purpose of preparing a new code of Indian law. Elected M.P. for Edinburgh, 1839. Lost his seat in 1847, but again represented Edinburgh in 1852-56. Raised to the peerage in 1857. Published the first of his famous essays, on "Milton," in "The Edinburgh Review," 1825; "Lays of Ancient Rome," 1842. The first two volumes of his "History of England" appeared in 1848. Died in 1859 at Campden Hill, and was buried in Westminster Abbey.

"It is hard to say whether his poetry, his speeches in Parliament, or his more brilliant essays, are the most charming; each has raised him to very great eminence."

Painted by Sir Francis Grant, P.R.A.

PLATE XXXI.

JAMES HENRY LEIGH HUNT, Poet and Essayist. Born at Southgate, 1784, son of the Rev. Isaac Hunt. Educated at Christ's Hospital. Founded the "Examiner" in 1808, for articles in which he was imprisoned and fined. Married Marianne Kent, 1809. His "Juvenalia" were published when he was 16 years old. Author of "The Story of Rimini," 1816; "Captain Sword and Captain Pen," 1835; his "Autobiography," 1850; and much in prose and verse. A close friend of Byron, Keats, Shelley, Lamb, Moore, Dickens, and Carlyle. Died at Putney, 1859, and buried at Kensal Green.

"His style, in spite of its mannerism, nay, partly by reason of its mannerism, is well suited for light, garrulous, desultory *ana*, half critical, half biographical."

"There is hardly a man living (1841) whose merits have been so grudgingly allowed, and whose faults have been so cruelly expiated."

Painted by Benjamin Robert Haydon.

PLATE XXXII.

THOMAS DE QUINCEY, author. Born at Manchester, 1785; fifth son of Thomas de Quincey. Educated at Salford, Bath, Linkfield and Manchester Grammar School, and Worcester College, Oxford, 1803-1807. It was during his residence at the University that he contracted the habit of opium eating, with which his memory is so intimately associated. He joined the band of poets known as "The Lakists," in 1809, and rapidly made a reputation as an essayist. "The Confessions of an English Opium Eater," after appearing in the "London Magazine," was published in collected form in 1822. Married Margaret Simpson, 1816. The "Logic of Political Economy" appeared, 1844. Died, 1859, and was buried in the West Churchyard of Edinburgh.

"De Quincey's writings range over a vast field of literary and semi-philosophical speculation and discussion; and there, as well as in his narrative, historical, critical and biographical essays, almost faultless refinement of style and marvellous mastery of phrase are conspicuous and charming."

Painted by J. Watson Gordon, P.R.S.A.

PLATE XXXIII.

ADMIRAL SIR JOHN ROSS, C.B., Arctic Explorer. Born at Balsarrock, Wigtonshire, 1777. Fourth son of Rev. Andrew Ross, of Inch. Entered the Navy, 1786. Set out in 1818, in company with Sir Edward Parry, to endeavour to make the North-West Passage. He made a second attempt in 1829. He was knighted on his return four years later. Was British Consul at Stockholm, 1839 to 1846. In 1850 went in search of Sir John Franklin. Became a rear-admiral in 1851. Died at his house in Gillingham Street, Pimlico, 1856.

"For that quality—essentially British—which we call "pluck," few names will stand out more clearly in the annals of Arctic exploration than that of Ross."

Painted in 1833, by James Green.

PLATE XXXIV.

SIR HENRY ROWLEY BISHOP, Musical Composer. Born in London, 1786. Studied under Francesco Bianchi. Made his first important success with "The Circassian Bride" (1809), and followed this with "The Knight of Snowdoun," 1811; "The Miller and His Men," 1813; "Guy Mannering," 1816; "The Law of Java" (with its popular "Mynheer Vandunck,") 1822; "Maid Marian," 1822; "Clari" (with its famous melody "Home, Sweet Home,") 1823; "The Fortunate Isles," 1840. Among his songs none is so popular, perhaps, as " My Pretty Jane." Conducted at Covent Garden from 1810 until 1840, with some intervals. Musical Director at Vauxhall, 1830-33. Knighted, 1842. Succeeded Dr. Crotch at Oxford, 1848. Died in London, 1855, and was buried at Finchley.

"Considering the time in which he lived, Bishop was a composer of more than average merit: always graceful, seldom uninteresting and never vulgar, he deserves a very high place among our native musicians. "Home, Sweet Home" may not be a great musical triumph, but it found its way directly to the heart of a nation."

Painter unknown.

PLATE XXXV.

SIR WILLIAM EDWARD PARRY, F.R.S., Arctic Explorer. Born at Bath, 1790. Fourth son of Dr. C. Hillier Parry. Entered the Navy in 1803, and served under Sir John Ross in 1818, and in 1819 commanded the "Hecla" in search of the North-West Passage. Returned to the Arctic Regions in 1821-3 and 1823-5. Made an attempt to reach the North Pole in sledge-boats in 1827. Knighted, 1829. Raised to rank of Rear-admiral of the White, 1852. Lieut.-governor of Greenwich Hospital, 1853. Died at Ems, in Germany, 1855, and was buried at Greenwich Hospital.

"He was worthy of his work: a pious, simple, straightforward, resolute man—a man in whose presence, it was said, 'trifles died a natural death'—made of the true material of which English great men have always been made."

Painted by S. Pearce in 1850.

PLATE XXXVI.

ARTHUR WELLESLEY, DUKE OF WELLINGTON, K.G., Soldier and Politician. Born in Dublin, or at Dangan Castle, Meath, 1769. Fifth son of Richard, first Earl of Mornington. Educated at Eton, in Brussels, and at the military seminary of Angers, in France. Gazetted ensign in the 41st Regiment, 1787, and joined in Dublin. Became captain in the 12th Lancers, 1791 ; major in the 33rd Foot, 1793 ; and lieutenant-colonel commanding the same year. First campaign in Flanders, 1794. Served with distinction in India, 1797-1805. Commander-in-chief of British forces in the Peninsula, 1808 to 1814, gaining numerous famous victories. Returned to England and passed through every grade of the peerage at one and the same time—saluted in succession " Baron," "Viscount," " Earl," " Marquis," and " Duke," and was presented with £400,000. Napoleon returned to France, 1st March, 1815. Wellington appointed to command the army in Belgium, and completely defeated Napoleon at Waterloo. Returned to England, 1818, and accepted post of Master General of the Ordnance. His last military operation was to concert measures for the defence of London against the Chartists in 1848. From 1842 to his death was commander-in-chief of the army. Became Prime Minister in 1828, resigning in 1830 over the Reform Bill. On the sudden dissolution of the Melbourne Ministry in 1834, Wellington undertook to discharge the whole duties of administration until Sir Robert Peel could return from abroad. He was again a member of the Cabinet in 1841. Died at Walmer Castle, 1852, and was buried in St. Paul's Cathedral.

> Great in council and great in war,
> Foremost captain of our time,
> Rich in seeming common sense,
> And as the greatest only are,
> In his simplicity sublime.

Painted by Count Alfred d'Orsay in 1845.

PLATE XXXVII.

WILLIAM WORDSWORTH, Poet. Born at Cockermouth, 1770, second son of John Wordsworth, attorney-at-law and law agent to Sir James Lowther, afterwards Earl of Lonsdale. Educated at Hawkshead and St. John's College, Cambridge, 1787-1791. Was in France during the Revolution. Settled at Grasmere in the Lake District, 1799. Married Miss Mary Hutchinson, 1803, settled at

Rydal Mount, 1813. Published "An Evening Walk," 1793; "Lyrical Ballads," 1798; "Poems," 1807; "The River Duddon," and other poems, 1820; "Description of the Scenery of the Lakes in the North of England," 1822; "Yarrow Revisited, and other poems," 1835; "The Prelude," 1850. Succeeded Southey as poet-laureate, 1843. Died at Rydal Mount, 1850.

"He had no masters but nature and solitude. 'He wrote a poem,' says Landor, 'without the aid of war.' His voice is the voice of sanity in a worldly and ambitious age. One regrets that his temperament was not more liquid and musical. He had written longer than he was inspired, but, for the rest, he has no competitor."

Drawn at the age of 28 by Robert Hancock.

Plate XXXVIII

SIR MARC ISAMBARD BRUNEL, Civil Engineer. Born at Hacqueville, in Normandy, 1769. Educated at Rouen. In 1786 became a sailor in the French navy. On the outbreak of the French Revolution established himself as a civil engineer at New York, 1793. Came to England, and married Miss Sophia Kingdom, in 1799. Introduced his plan for producing ship blocks by machinery at Portsmouth Dockyard. Did much to advance steam navigation, but is best known as the engineer of the Thames Tunnel, which was commenced under the auspices of the Duke of Wellington in 1825, and opened for traffic in 1843. Elected F.R.S. in 1814, and appointed Vice-President in 1832. He was knighted in 1841, and died in 1849. Buried at Kensal Green.

"In fertility of resource, perseverance, combined with untiring energy under adverse circumstances may be found the secret of his success."

Painted by James Northcote, R.A., in 1813.

Plate XXXIX.

GEORGE STEPHENSON, Engineer. Second son of Robert Stephenson, a colliery fireman, born at Wylam, Northumberland, 1781. Was the father of railways, being the first to apply the locomotive steam engine to railways for passenger traffic. Married Frances Henderson, 1802; Elizabeth Hindmarsh, 1820; Miss Gregory, 1848. In 1815 he patented his first locomotive, the

"Blutcher," made at Killingworth, and constructed his first railway at Hetton. He next planned the line from Stockton to Darlington, and subsequently that between Liverpool and Manchester, which was opened in 1830. The "Rocket" made its first successful trial in 1829. He was chief engineer to most of the lines of railway made during the succeeding ten years. He died at Tapton, Derbyshire, 1848, and was buried in Trinity Church, Chesterfield.

"The leading feature of his mind was honesty of purpose, and determination in carrying it out. Towards trickery and affectation he never concealed his contempt, while honest merit never appealed to his liberality in vain."

Painted by Henry W. Pickersgill, R.A.

PLATE XL.

REAR-ADMIRAL SIR JOHN FRANKLIN, Arctic Explorer. Youngest son of Willingham Franklin. Born at Spilsby, Lincolnshire, 1786. Educated at St. Ives and Louth Grammar School. Entered the Navy, 1801, and was present at the battles of Copenhagen and Trafalgar. Made his first voyage to the Arctic regions in "The Trent," 1818, and revisited the Polar regions in 1825. Elected F.R.S. 1822. Married Miss Porden, 1823; Miss Griffin, 1828. Lieutenant Governor of Van Diemen's Land from 1836 to 1843, and in the early part of 1845 set out with the "Erebus" and "Terror" in search of the North-West Passage. Nothing was heard of the Expedition after July of this year until "The Fox," fitted out by Lady Franklin and commanded by Sir Leopold McClintock, discovered in 1859 evidence pointing to the loss of the expedition and the death of Franklin on June 11th, 1847, after having discovered, but not actually traversed, the North-West Passage.

"He was one of the boldest and most persevering explorers that Britain has ever sent from her shores. His daring was qualified by judgment, and his sense of duty and responsibility as to the lives of those under his charge was of the keenest. His heart was tender as a woman's; and altogether he was one of the noblest types of a true Christian gentleman."

Painted by Thomas Phillips, R.A.

PLATE XLI.

DANIEL O'CONNELL, M.P., "The Liberator," Politician and Orator. Eldest son of Morgan O'Connell. Born at Carhen House, Cahirciveen, in Co. Kerry, 1775. Educated under Father Harrington, at Cove, and at the colleges of St. Omar and Douay.

Entered Lincoln's Inn, 1794, and was called to the Bar four years later. Married his cousin Mary, 1802. Elected M.P. for Co. Clare in 1828, and did much to secure the introduction and passing of the Roman Catholic Emancipation Act in 1829. Became famous as an orator and for the vigour of his agitation for the repeal of the Union. Died at Genoa, 1847, and buried at Glasnevin, Ireland.

"His position in history is unique. Few other men have possessed his personal influence, and no other man has used such influence with greater moderation and self-abnegation.

Painted on Ivory in 1836 by Bernard Mulrenin, R.H.A.

PLATE XLII.

THOMAS HOOD, Poet and Humorist. Second son of Thomas Hood, a bookseller. Born in the Poultry, London, 1799. Educated privately. Began life in a merchant's office and was afterwards apprenticed to his uncle, an engraver, by whom he was transferred to Le Keux. Abandoned engraving for literature. Sub-edited the "London Magazine," 1821; issued his "Whims and Oddities," 1826-27; commenced his "Comic Annual," 1830; wrote "The Dream of Eugene Aram"; "Epping Hunt," 1834; "Tylney Hall," 1834; "The Song of the Shirt," 1843; succeeded Theodore Hook as editor of the "New Monthly Magazine," 1841, in which appeared "Miss Kilmansegg." Died in London, 1845, and buried at Kensal Green.

"He sang the Song of the Shirt."

Painter uncertain.

PLATE XLIII.

ROBERT SOUTHEY, LL.D., Poet Laureate. Son of a linendraper. Born at Bristol, 1774. Entered Westminster School, 1788, and Balliol College, Oxford, 1792. After travelling in Spain; married Edith Fricker, 1795; settled at Keswick, in Cumberland, 1803. Wrote "Joan of Arc," 1795; "Thalaba," 1801; "Madoc," 1805; "The Curse of Kehama," 1810; "Roderick, the Last of the Goths," 1814; "The Life of John Wesley," 1820;

"A Vision of Judgment," 1821; "The History of Brazil," 1810-19; "History of the Peninsular War," 1823-30; "Naval History of England," 1833-40. Died at Keswick, 1843, and buried in Crosthwaite Churchyard.

"His prose is perfect. Of his poetry there are various opinions; there is, perhaps, too much for the present generation; posterity will probably select. He has *passages* equal to anything."

Drawn in 1804 by Henry Edridge, A.R.A.

PLATE XLIV.

THOMAS ARNOLD, D.D., Head Master of Rugby. Born at East Cowes, 1795. Educated at Warminster and Winchester. Entered Corpus Christi College, Oxford, 1811; took a first-class in classics, 1814, and elected Fellow of Oriel, 1815. Married Mary Penrose, 1820. Became Head Master of Rugby, 1828, which school, under his direction, became one of the most celebrated seats of learning of the time. Appointed Regius Professor of Modern History at Oxford, 1841. His views on education were published in "The Journal of Education," 1834-5, and he published a "Roman History," in three volumes, 1838-43. Died at Rugby, 1842, and was buried in the School Chapel.

"Strong, hopeful, helpful soul, cheering and supporting his weaker comrades on their upward and onward way."

A marble bust sculptured in 1849 by W. Behnes.

PLATE XLV.

GRACE HORSLEY DARLING, Heroine. Daughter of the keeper of a lighthouse in the Farne Islands. Born at Bamborough, 1815. Her name is famous in connection with the wreck of the s.s. "Forfarshire," on September 7th, 1838, when Grace Darling rowed an open boat with her father to the rocks, and rescued four men and one woman. She received the Royal Humane Society's Gold Medal. Died of consumption, 1842, and buried at Bamborough.

Marble bust by D. Dunbar.

PLATE XLVI.

THEODORE EDWARD HOOK, Author and Wit. Son of James Hook, composer. Born in London, 1788, and educated at Harrow. Attracted notice by the success of a slight opera, "The Soldier's Return," 1804. Appointed Accountant-General and Treasurer of the Mauritius, 1812, but returned in 1819. Became editor of the "John Bull," 1820. His best known works are:— "Sayings and Doings" (1826-29), "Maxwell" (1830), "Love and Pride" (1832), "Jack Brag" (1836), and "Births, Marriages, and Deaths" (1839). Obtained a great reputation as a wit, and is one of the few Englishmen who attained the art of improvisation in poetry. Died at Fulham in 1841.

"His real tastes were simple enough; he was humane, charitable, and generous. There was that about him, which made it hard to be often in his society without regarding him with as much of fondness as of admiration."

Painted by Eden Upton Eddis.

PLATE XLVII.

SIR DAVID WILKIE, R.A., Genre Painter. Son of the minister of Cults, Fifeshire. Born in his father's parish, 1785. Went to Edinburgh, 1799, and came to the Royal Academy Schools, London, 1805. Painted the "Village Politicians," 1806. Travelled in Italy and Spain, 1824, and returned to England, 1828. Succeeded Sir Thomas Lawrence as Painter in Ordinary to Her Majesty, 1830, and was knighted 1836. Went to the East, 1840, but died off Gibraltar on his way home, 1841.

"I will find you a young Scotsman who is second to no Dutchman who ever bore a palette on his thumb."

"Wilkie is the Goldsmith of painters, in the amiable and pathetic humour, in the combination of smiles and tears, of the familiar and the beautiful. He is the exact illustration of the power and dignity of the popular school in the hands of a master."

Painted by himself in 1814.

PLATE XLVIII.

JOHN CONSTABLE, R.A., Landscape Painter. Second child of Golding Constable. Born at East Bergholt, Suffolk, 1776. Educated at Lavenham and Dedham. Came to London 1795; and entered at the Royal Academy Schools, 1799. One of the founders of the school of English landscape painters, and one of the greatest painters of that school. "The Hay Wain," "The Cornfield," and "The Valley Farm," are in the National Gallery, and the "Salisbury Cathedral" at the South Kensington Museum. He was elected A.R.A. in 1819 and a Royal Academician, 1829. Married Maria Bicknell, 1816. Died in London, 1837, and buried at Hampstead.

"He was the most genuine painter of English cultivated scenery, leaving untouched its mountains and lakes."

"His works are to be deeply respected as thoroughly original, thoroughly honest, free from affectation, manly in manner, frequently successful in cool colour, and realizing certain motives of English scenery, with perhaps as much affection as such scenery, unless where regarded through media of feeling derived from higher sources, is calculated to inspire."

Drawn by himself in lead pencil and tinted.

PLATE XLIX.

JOSEPH GRIMALDI, Pantomimist. Son of Guiseppe Grimaldi, a Genoese, who came to England as dentist to Queen Charlotte, but relinquished that position to become ballet-master of Old Drury Lane and Sadlers' Wells Theatres. Born in London, 1779, and first appeared on the stage at Sadlers' Wells when two years old. Appeared as clown at Drury Lane and Covent Garden Theatres. Retired in 1832. Died in London, 1837, and was buried in the cemetery of St. James's Chapel, Pentonville.

"As a clown, Grimaldi is held to have had no equal. His grimace was inexpressibly mirth-moving, and with him the days of genuine pantomine drollery are held to have expired."

Painted by John Cawse.

PLATE L.

REV. EDWARD IRVING, M.A., Divine and Preacher. Son of Gavin Irving, a tanner. Born at Annan in Dumfrieshire, 1792. Educated at Annan Day School and Edinburgh University. Obtained the mastership of Haddington Mathematical School, and afterwards that of Kirkcaldy. He came to London in 1822 and was appointed minister to a chapel connected with the Caledonian Asylum. He attracted a crowded congregation by the eloquence of his preaching, but in his published sermons and orations he enunciated such views as led to his expulsion from the Scottish church. Married Isabella Martin, 1823. He established an independent sect, 1832, and founded the "Holy Catholic Apostolic Church," the first meetings being held in Benjamin West's old picture gallery in Newman Street. The present cathedral of the body is in Gordon Square. Died at Glasgow, 1834, and buried in Glasgow Cathedral.

"He was one of the most striking figures in ecclesiastical history, and as exempt from every taint of charlatanism as a man can be. His life was a succession of tender and charitable actions, in so far as his polemics left him time and opportunity."

Drawn by Joseph Slater.

PLATE LI.

CHARLES LAMB, Essayist. Son of John Lamb, a barrister's clerk. Born in Crown Office Row, in the Temple, 1775. Went to Christ's Hospital from 1782 to 1789. Spent two years in the South Sea House; but obtained a seat in the Accountant's office of the East India Company, 1792, and remained there until 1825. At the age of twenty-one spent some weeks in the Hoxton Lunatic Asylum. In 1796 the great tragedy of his life befel him, his sister Mary was attacked with homicidal mania, and henceforward Charles Lamb devoted his life to her care. Published, conjointly with his schoolfellows, S. T. Coleridge and Lloyd, his first poems in 1797. His "Tales from Shakespeare" were published in 1807; "Specimens of English Dramatic Poets" in 1808, and in 1818 his "Works" were collected and published. In 1820 "The London Magazine" was established and in its columns first appeared "The Essays of Elia." The latter essays were published in volume form in 1833. Died and buried at Edmonton, 1834.

"An occasional intoxication, which hurt no one but himself, which blinded him to no duty, which led him into no extravagance, which in no way interfered with the soundness of his judgment, the charity of his heart, or the independence of his life, and a shower of bad puns—behold the faults of Elia! His virtues—noble, manly, gentle—are strewn over every page of his life, and may be read in every letter he wrote."

Painted in 1805 by William Hazlitt.

PLATE LII.

JOHN O'KEEFFE, Dramatist and Actor. Born in Dublin, 1747. Originally intended for an artist. Entered the Royal Hibernian Academy when six years old. Educated by Father Austin. Began his career as an actor under Mossop at Dublin, and wrote his first comedy, "The Gallant," when he was only 15. Established himself in London, 1780. His best known plays are "The Agreeable Surprise," "The Lie of the Day," "Castle of Andalusia," "Wild Oats," "Peeping Tom." His eyesight began to fail in his twenty-third year, culminating in complete blindness about 1797. Twenty-one of his sixty-eight pieces were published in four volumes in 1798. Died and buried at Southampton, 1833.

"He was always a facile, if not a finished writer."

Painted in 1786 by Thomas Lawranson.

PLATE LIII.

WILLIAM WILBERFORCE, M.P., Statesman and Philanthropist. His father was a wealthy merchant, descended from an old family, proprietors of Wilberfoss, in the East Riding of Yorks. Born at Hull, 1759. Educated at Wimbledon and Pocklington, Yorks., and St John's College, Cambridge, 1776. Elected M.P. for Hull, 1780; for Yorkshire, 1784, and for Boramber, 1812. Chiefly famous for his exertions, in association with Granville Sharp and Thomas Clarkson, to obtain the abolition of the slave trade, which great object may be said to have been accomplished in 1804, after a powerful opposition extending over fifteen years. His "Practical View of the Prevailing Religious System of Professed Christians" was published in 1797. Retired from public life, 1825, and died at Cadogan Place, 1833. Buried in Westminster Abbey.

"I never saw one who touched life at so many points."

An unfinished portrait by Sir Thomas Lawrence, P.R.A.

PLATE LIV.

SIR WALTER SCOTT, BART., Novelist and Poet. Fourth surviving child of Walter Scott, Writer to the Signet. Born at Edinburgh, 1771. Educated at Edinburgh High School, 1778, and Edinburgh University, 1783-4. Called to the bar, 1792. Married Miss Carpenter, 1797. Became Sheriff of Selkirkshire, 1799; appointed one of the principal Clerks of the Quarter Session, 1806. Produced "Lay of the Last Minstrel," 1805; "Marmion," 1808; "The Lady of the Lake," 1810; "The Lord of the Isles," 1815. "Waverley" was published anonymously, 1814, and the rest of the Waverley Novels between this date and 1832. The secret of the authorship of these novels was not publicly admitted until 1827, when "the derangement of the affairs of my publishers and the exposure of their account books, which was the natural consequence, rendered secrecy no longer possible." Created a baronet at Holyrood, 1820. Died at Abbotsford, 1832, and buried at Dryburgh Abbey.

"As a writer it is a truism to say that, since Shakespeare, whom he resembled in many ways, there has never been a genius so human and so creative, so rich in humour, sympathy, poetry, so fertile in the production of new and real characters as the genius of Sir Walter Scott."

Painted in 1832, by Sir William Allan, R.A.

PLATE LV.

PATRICK NASMYTH, Landscape Painter. Son of Alexander Nasmyth. Born in Edinburgh, 1787, but when about twenty settled in London. Exhibited at the Royal Academy from 1809, and was one of the original members of the Society of British Artists. His life was one of solitude and suffering, "from which he sought refuge in strong drink, as well as in the beauties of nature." He died at Lambeth, 1831.

"He painted by preference the footpaths, hedges, common pasture ground, and dwarf oaks of the outskirts of London."

He painted, it has been said, "with absolute fidelity."

Drawn by William Bewick.

PLATE LVI.

SARAH SIDDONS, Tragic Actress. Daughter of Roger Kemble. Born at Brecon, South Wales, 1755. Introduced upon the stage as an infant phenomenon, and when 13 performed principally as a vocalist. Resided from 1772 to 1779 "as companion" to Mrs. Greathead, of Guy's Cliff, Warwickshire. Married William Siddons, a young actor, 1773, and returned with him to the stage. Appeared as *Portia* in London, 1775, with Garrick as *Shylock*. Reappeared at Drury Lane as *Isabella*, in "The Fatal Marriage," 1782. Her principal parts were *Lady Macbeth, Constance* in "King John," *Queen Katherine*, and *Lady Randolph* in "Douglas." Retired from the stage, 1812. Died in London, 1831, and buried in Paddington churchyard.

"As a tragic actress, Mrs. Siddons has probably in this country never been equalled; as a woman she was of unblemished reputation, and enjoyed the respect of all who knew her."

Painted in 1798, by Sir William Beechey, R.A.

PLATE LVII.

WILLIAM BLAKE, Poet, Artist, Engraver. Son of a hosier. Born in London, 1757. Learnt drawing at Paris. Apprenticed to Basire, a well-known engraver. With the assistance of Flaxman, the sculptor, and a Mr. Matthews, he published a volume of poems when he was 30. "Songs of Innocence" appeared in 1789; his illustrations to Young's "Night Thoughts," 1779; the "Turloe Inventions" in illustration of "Blair's Grave," 1808; and his twenty-one "Inventions for the Book of Job," 1820. Exhibited pictures at the R.A. between 1780 and 1808. Died at Fountain Court, Strand, 1827.

"I was sent into this world not to gather gold, but to make glorious shapes expressing God-like sentiments."

Painted by Thomas Phillips, R.A.

PLATE LVIII.

REV. SAMUEL PARR, LL.D., Greek Scholar. Son of a surgeon. Born at Harrow, 1747. Educated at Harrow and Emmanuel College, Cambridge. Accepted an assistant-mastership at Harrow, 1767. Appointed Master of Colchester School, 1777, and of Norwich School, 1778. Settled at Hatton, Warwickshire, 1786, where he spent the rest of his life. Appointed Rector of Graffham, Huntingdonshire, 1790. Died and buried at Hatton, 1825.

"He was an amazing, an overwhelming talker. Bold, dogmatic, arrogant, with a memory profoundly and minutely retentive, and with a genuine gift of ephemeral epigram, he seemed at the tables of statesmen, and wits, and divines, to be a man of tremendous talent, capable of any literary feat; but the learning and repartee have left little trace of their existence, and posterity declines to admire the wonders that it has neither seen nor heard."

Painted by George Dawe, R.A.

PLATE LIX.

GEORGE GORDON (Sixth LORD BYRON), Poet. Born in London, 1788. Son of John Byron and Catherine Gordon, a Scottish heiress of ancient and illustrious extraction. Inherited his title and large though embarrassed estates from his grand-uncle, in his eleventh year. Was sent at the age of five to a day-school in Aberdeen. Thence he went to Harrow, and Trinity College, Cambridge. While at Cambridge he published "Hours of Idleness, by Lord Byron, a Minor." The savage attack upon this in the *Edinburgh Review*, produced in reply "English Bards and Scotch Reviewers." The first two cantos of "Childe Harold" appeared in 1812-13, and was followed in rapid succession by "The Giaour," "The Bride of Abydos," "The Corsair," and "Lara." He travelled much in Italy, Greece, Turkey and the East, and produced the third canto of "Childe Harold," 1816; "The Prisoner of Chillon," 1816; "Manfred," 1816; and "The Lament of Tasso," 1817; "Mazeppa," 1819; the first five cantos of "Don Juan," and most of his tragedies, appeared between 1818 and 1821. Joined the Greek patriotic movement, 1824, and died of marsh fever at Missolonghi, 1824, and buried at Hucknall Torkard.

"The grand Napoleon of the realms of rhyme."

Painted by Richard Westall, in 1825, a replica.

PLATE LX.

EDWARD JENNER, M.D., F.R.S. The discoverer of vaccination. Born in Berkeley, Gloucestershire, 1749. Son of Rev. Stephen Jenner, Rector of Rockhampton. Educated at Cirencester, and apprenticed to Mr. Ludlow, an eminent surgeon at Sodbury, near Bristol. Went to London, 1760, and studied under the celebrated John Hunter at St. George's Hospital. Returned to Berkeley, 1773. Obtained the degree of M.D. from the University of St. Andrew's, 1792. Discovered the prophylactic power of vaccination, 1796, and published his first memoir on the subject, 1798. Parliament voted him a grant of £10,000 in 1802, and £20,000 in 1807. Died and buried at Berkeley, 1823.

"With deep and anxious emotion he mentioned his hope of being able to propagate that variety of disease from one human being to another, till he had disseminated the practice all over the globe, to the total extinction of small-pox."

Painted by James Northcote, R.A.

PLATE LXI.

SIR WILLIAM HERSCHEL, F.R.S., Astronomer. Born at Hanover, 1738. Son of a musician, and educated for the same profession. Joined the band of the Hanoverian Foot Guards, 1752, and came to England, 1757. Became teacher of music at Leeds, and subsequently organist at Halifax and at Bath. Discovered the planet Uranus, 1780. Appointed private astronomer to George III.; received the Guelphic Order of Knighthood. Devoted the remainder of his life to astronomy. Greatly added to the knowledge of the solar system, and first perceived the rotation of Saturn's ring. Announced, in 1803, the motion of binary stars round one another. Erected a monster telescope at Slough, 1785-87. Died at Slough, 1822, and buried at Upton.

" He was the first to give the human mind any conception of the immensity of the universe. His is one of the few names which belong to the whole world."

Painted by Lemuel F. Abbott, 1785.

PLATE LXII.

JAMES WATT, Mechanician, Engineer, and Scientist. Son of a blockmaker and general merchant at Greenock, in Scotland. Born at Greenock, 1736. Studied at home, and was sent to London to learn the trade of a mathematical instrument-maker, 1754. Appointed instrument-maker to Glasgow University, 1757. Employed in surveying the Clyde and Forth Canal, 1767. Began experiments on the properties of steam, and improvements in machinery, 1763. Took out a patent for his steam-engine, 1769. Retired from business, 1800. Died at Heathfield, in Staffordshire, 1819.

" Directing the force of an original genius, early exercised in philosophical research, to the improvement of the steam-engine, he enlarged the resources of his country, increased the power of man, and rose to an eminent place amongst the most illustrious followers of science, and the real benefactors of the world."

Painted by Charles F. de Bredda, 1793.

PLATE LXIII.

RIGHT HON. WARREN HASTINGS, first Governor General of India. Born in the West Indies, 1732. Son of Pynaston Hastings. Left an orphan and educated at Daylesford,

Newington and Westminster (where he met Elijah Impey), and in 1750 sailed for Bengal and entered the service of the East India Company. Was employed at Cossimbazar, imprisoned at Moorshedabad during the Mutiny, was relieved by Clive and appointed diplomatic agent to the Nabob of Bengal. Became a Member of Council, 1761, and resided in Calcutta. Returned to England, 1764. Appointed Member of Council at Madras, 1766. Placed at the head of the Government of Bengal, 1772, and made Governor-general of all British India, 1774, and remained at the head of the government of Bengal till the spring of 1785. His administration, so eventful and stormy, closed in almost perfect peace. He returned to England and was impeached by the House of Commons in 1786. He was arrested by the Serjeant-at-arms. The sittings of the court commenced in 1788, in Westminster Hall, and continued for seven years. He was acquitted by a large majority, 1795. He was a ruined man. The East India Company, however, granted him an annuity and he retired into private life, residing at Daylesford, Worcestershire. In 1813 he gave evidence at the Bar of the House, and was sworn of the Privy Council in 1814. He died and was buried at Daylesford in 1818.

"We cannot regard without admiration the amplitude and fertility of his intellect, his rare talents for command, for administration and controversy, his dauntless courage, his honourable poverty, his fervent zeal for the interests of the State, his noble equanimity, tried by both extremes of fortune, and never disturbed by either."

A bronze bust sculptured by Thomas Banks, R.A., in 1794.

PLATE LXIV.

MATTHEW GREGORY LEWIS, M.P., Romance Writer and Dramatist. Son of Matthew Lewis, Deputy Secretary for War. Born in London, 1775. Educated at the school of Dr. Fountaine and at Westminster. Afterwards attended at a German university. Obtained a seat in Parliament for Hindon. Author of "The Monk," "Tales of Wonder," and "The Castle Spectre." Died and buried at sea whilst returning from Jamaica in 1818.

"He looked like a school-boy all his life, and retained many of the qualities of a precocious and ill-educated school-boy."

Painted by H. W. Pickersgill, R.A.

PLATE LXV.

JOHN PHILPOT CURRAN, Orator. Born at Newmarket, Co. Cork, Ireland, 1750. Educated at Trinity College, Dublin. Entered the Middle Temple, 1773. Called to the Irish Bar, 1775. Elected member for Kilbeggan in the Irish Parliament, 1783. Was in favour of the formation of Irish Volunteers, 1788. Warmly opposed the Union. Appointed Master of the Rolls in Ireland, 1806, which office he resigned in 1814. Died in London, 1817.

"Curran is best remembered for his wit and gaiety; to his humorous, flowery and sarcastic speech must be attributed his success, which his attractive social qualities did much to extend."

Painted in the style of Wm. Owen, R.A.

PLATE LXVI.

RIGHT HON. RICHARD BRINSLEY SHERIDAN, M.P., Politician, Dramatist and Orator. Born in Dublin, 1751. Son of Thomas Sheridan, actor. Educated at Harrow and at the Middle Temple. "The Rivals" was produced in 1775; "St. Patrick's Day," 1775; "The Duenna," 1775; "The School for Scandal," 1777; "The Critic," 1779. He was returned to Parliament for Stafford in 1780, and for thirty-one years was an active and useful member of the House of Commons. He was appointed Secretary to the Treasury in 1783. His famous "Begum" speech was delivered in 1787. He was twice married. He died in hopeless distress in Savile Row, 1816, and was buried with princely pomp in Westminster Abbey.

Byron justly said that the intellectual reputation of Sheridan was truly enviable, that he had made the best speech, that on the Begums of Oude; written the two best comedies, "The Rivals" and "The School for Scandal"; the best opera, "The Duenna"; and the best farce, "The Critic."

"Our Incomparable Brinsley."

Drawn in Crayon by John Russell, R.A., 1788.

PLATE LXVII.

EMMA, LADY HAMILTON. Second wife of Sir William Hamilton, K.B., British Ambassador at Naples. Born, 1761; married, 1791. Confidante of Queen Caroline of Naples, and friend of Lord Nelson. Noted for her beauty. Died at Calais, 1815.

Painted by George Romney.

PLATE LXVIII.

CHARLES DIBDIN, Musician, Song-writer and Actor. Born at Southampton, 1745. Son of Thomas Dibdin, parish clerk. Educated at Winchester, and placed under Fussell, the organist of the Cathedral. Came to London, and "The Shepherd's Artifice" was produced at Covent Garden Theatre when he was but 16. Appeared as an actor in his own farce, "The Padlock," 1768. Became musical director of Covent Garden Theatre, 1778, and built the Circus (now known as the Surrey Theatre), 1782. The "Musical Tour" was published in 1788, and the popular entertainments entitled "The Whim of the Moment," commenced in 1789. His patriotic sea songs obtained for him a pension of £200 a year from the Government. He died and was buried at Camden Town, 1814.

"Neptune, and not Apollo, seems to have inspired him."

Painted in 1799, by Thomas Philips, R.A.

PLATE LXIX.

RT. HON. CHAS. JAMES FOX, M.P., Statesman. Son of Henry Fox, first Lord Holland. Born in Conduit Street, 1749. Educated at Eton and Oxford. Elected M.P. for Midhurst, 1768. Held several subordinate offices under Lord North's administration, but afterwards joined the Opposition Benches. Vigorously opposed the coercive measures adopted by the government with regard to the American Colonies. Appointed Secretary of State, 1782. Formed his famous coalition with Lord North, 1783, which was soon displaced by Mr. Pitt's administration. Was a strenuous opponent of the war with France, and was recalled to office after the death of Pitt, 1806. Died at Chiswick, 1806, and was buried in Westminster Abbey.

"The greatest debater the world ever saw, and the most Demosthenian speaker since Demosthenes."

Painted by Karl Anton Hickel, in 1793.

PLATES LXX. AND LXXI.

HORATIO, VISCOUNT NELSON. Son of the Rev. Edmund Nelson, of Burnham Thorpe, Norfolk, where he was born, 1758. Entered the navy at the age of 13 as midshipman on the "Raisonnable," under his uncle, Captain Suckling. Appointed post-captain, 1779. Invested with the Order of the Bath, 1797. Achieved the splendid victory of the Nile over the French fleet, 1798. Shattered the naval power of Denmark at Copenhagen, 1801. Annihilated the French fleet at Trafalgar, 1805, in which battle he was mortally wounded. Buried in St. Paul's Cathedral, 1806.

"In coolness, foresight, promptitude, instant tuition, decision, and a daring which, even when it seemed at times to border on temerity, was yet regulated throughout by the nicest calculations of reason, he has perhaps never been quite equalled on the element."

1. Painted by Heinrich Füger, 1800 (unfinished).
2. ,, Lemuel Francis Abbott.

PLATE LXXII.

GEORGE ROMNEY, Artist. Born at Becleside, Dalton-in-Furness, 1734. Son of "honest John Romney," a cabinet-maker. Showed talent in designing and wood-carving at an early age. Was apprenticed to Steele, an indifferent painter, at the age of 21. Married Mary Abbott, 1756. Went to London, 1762, where for ten years he met with varying success. He spent two years in Italy, and on his return to London established himself in Cavendish Square. He became the rival of Reynolds—who always referred to him as "the man in Cavendish Square"—and was never admitted into the ranks of the Royal Academicians. Besides his portraits he painted many large historical compositions. In 1796 he took a house at Hampstead, on Holly Bush Hill. Romney was the painter *par excellence* of Lady Hamilton, and forty portraits of her by him are still known. When old, nearly mad, and quite desolate, he went back to his wife, "to die at home at last," 1802.

"Romney wanted but education and reading to make him a very fine painter; but his ideal was not high nor fixed."

"Few artists since the fifteenth century, have been able to do so much in so many different branches."

Painted by himself, in December, 1782 (unfinished).

PLATE LXXIII.

GEORGE WASHINGTON, First President of the United States. Born in Westmoreland County, Virginia, 1732. Son of Augustine Washington and his second wife, Mary Ball. Obtained the office of Surveyor of the Western District of Virginia, 1750. Appointed adjutant of the provincial troops, with the rank of major, 1751, and commanded a regiment against the French, 1754. Selected to command the troops raised in Virginia, 1774, and in 1775 represented that state in the Convention at Philadelphia. Chosen commander-in-chief of the American forces against the mother country, 1775. Brought the war to a successful termination, and retired to Mount Vernon, 1783. Elected President and inaugurated at New York, 1789. Died, 1799.

"He was mourned even by his enemies, and deserved the record :—' First in peace, first in war, and first in the hearts of his countrymen.'"

Attributed to Gilbert Stuart.

PLATE LXXIV.

RT. HON. EDMUND BURKE, M.P., Philosopher and Statesman. Son of Richard Burke, an attorney. Born in Dublin, 1729. Educated at Ballitore, Co. Kildare, and at Trinity College, Dublin. Entered the Middle Temple, 1747. Became private secretary to the Marquis of Rockingham, 1765. Elected for Wendover, 1765, and for Malton, 1774. Twice appointed Paymaster-general of the Forces, and became a member of the Coalition Ministry, 1783. Took a prominent part in the trial of Warren Hastings, 1788. Vigorously opposed the government policy with regard to the American and Indian colonies. Retired from parliament, 1794. Published his "Philosophical Enquiry into the Origin of our Ideas on the Sublime and the Beautiful," 1756, and "Reflections on the French Revolution," 1790. Died and buried at Beaconsfield, 1797.

"He was a sort of power in Europe, though totally without any of those means, or the smallest share in them, which give or maintain power in other men."

Painted by Sir Joshua Reynolds, P.R.A.

Plate LXXV.

HORATIO ("HORACE") WALPOLE, Fourth Earl of Orford. Youngest son of Sir Robert Walpole, the Prime Minister. Born, 1717. Educated at Eton and King's College, Cambridge. Travelled abroad for some years with Gray, the poet, after finishing his education. Returned to England and was returned as member for Callington, 1741. Exchanged his seat for that of Castle Rising, 1744, and represented King's Lynn, 1754. Published his "Catalogue of Royal and Noble Authors," 1758; "Castle of Otranto," 1764; "Historic Doubts on the Life and Reign of Richard III." Best known by his epistolary correspondence. Became fourth Earl of Orford, 1791. Died 1797.

"The conformation of his mind was such that whatever was little seemed to him great, and whatever was great seemed to him little. Serious business was a trifle to him, and trifles were his serious business."

"The best letter writer in the English language."

Painted by Nathaniel Hone, R.A.

Plate LXXVI.

ROBERT BURNS, Poet. Born in the Hamlet of Alloway, in Ayrshire, 1759. Son of William Burness, a peasant farmer or gardener. He obtained an unusually sound education at the parish school of Dalrymple. In early life the immortal "Ayrshire ploughman" laboured upon his father's farm, and afterwards endeavoured, but without success, to conduct a farm with his brothers. It was in his seventeenth year that he first "committed the sin of rhyme;" but it was not until after his father's decease in 1784 that, in order to provide funds for his voyage to the West Indies—whither he had intended to emigrate—he published a collection of his poems by subscription. These were received with a tempest of enthusiasm that instantly made Burns the idol of the fashionable and literary world of Edinburgh. After again falling into financial embarrassments he obtained a humble appointment in the Excise service. In 1792, Burns composed new songs for a collection of Scottish national airs, and he continued to add to this collection until the last month of his brief life. His naturally strong constitution was undermined by excess and excitement of all kinds, and the poet died at Dumfries, in extreme poverty, in 1796.

"The greatest poet, beyond all comparison, that Scotland has produced."

"In Burns the highest and most apparently incompatible qualities were united to a degree which is rarely met with—tenderness the most exquisite, humour the broadest and the most refined, the most delicate and yet powerful perception of natural beauty, the highest finish and the easiest negligence of style. . . . . . . His writings are chiefly lyric."

Painted by Alexander Nasmyth.

PLATE LXXVII.

JOHN HUNTER, Surgeon and Anatomist. Born at Long Calderwood, Lanarkshire, 1728. Son of a farmer. Remained for seventeen years without education or definite occupation. Acted as assistant in his brother William's dissecting-room, 1748. Studied surgery under Cheselden at Chelsea Hospital, 1749-50, and subsequently under Pott. Entered St. Mary's Hall, Oxford, 1755. Elected F.R.S., 1767, and appointed surgeon to St. George's Hospital, 1768. Created surgeon-extraordinary to George III., 1776. Constructed a museum, 1783-85, containing over 10,000 specimens and preparations to illustrate comparative anatomy, physiology, and natural history. Appointed deputy-surgeon to the army, 1786, and received the Copley Medal from the Royal Society, 1787. Died, 1793, and was buried at St. Martin's-in-the-Fields, whence his remains were removed to Westminster Abbey, 1859.

"John Hunter—the greatest name in the combined character of physiologist and surgeon, that the whole annals of medicine can furnish."

Copied by John Jackson, R.A., in 1816, from Sir Joshua Reynolds, P.R.A.

PLATE LXXVIII.

SIR JOSHUA REYNOLDS, P.R.A., Artist. Born at Plympton-Earl's, Devonshire, 1723. Son of the Rev. Samuel Reynolds. Educated at the Plympton Grammar School. Sent to London, 1740, and placed under Hudson. Went abroad in 1749, and returned to England, 1752, and settled in St. Martin's Lane. Became the intimate friend of Dr. Johnson, Burke, and others, and on the foundation of the Royal Academy by George III., in 1768, was nominated president and knighted. He was made D.C.L. of Oxford, 1773. Between the years 1769 and 1790, Reynolds exhibited no less than 244 pictures. He was never married, and died in Leicester Fields, 1792, and was buried in St. Paul's Cathedral.

"Considered as a painter of individuality in the human form and mind, I think him the prince of portrait painters. Titian paints nobler pictures, and Van Dyck had nobler subjects, but neither of them entered so subtly as Sir Joshua did into the inner varieties of human heart and temper."

"The swiftest of painters and the gentlest of companions."

Painted by himself before his residence in Italy.

PLATE LXXIX.

JOHN SMEATON, F.R.S., Civil Engineer. Born at Austhorpe Lodge, near Leeds, 1724. Son of an attorney. At the age of 15 he constructed a machine for rose-engine turning. Removed to London, 1750, and started business in Holborn as an instrument maker. Became a member of the Royal Society, 1753. Gained the Copley Medal of the Royal Society, 1759, for improvements on millwork. Erected the Eddystone Lighthouse, 1757-1759. His other chief engineering works were: the construction of Ramsgate Harbour, the Forth and Clyde Canal, the erection of the Spurn Lighthouse, and of several important bridges in Scotland, together with an immense amount of mill machinery. Died at Austhorpe, 1792.

"His advice on difficult or important engineering schemes was invariably demanded, and almost always followed—a proof not only of his eminence in his profession, but of his caution, judgment and integrity."

Painted probably by Rhodes.

PLATE LXXX.

REV. JOHN WESLEY, M.A., the Founder of Methodism. Born at Epworth, 1703. Son of Rev. Samuel Wesley, rector of Epworth, Lincolnshire. Educated at Charterhouse and Christ Church, Oxford. Took his degree of M.A., was elected Fellow of Lincoln College, and ordained by Bishop Potter, in 1726. Joined the Society of the Methodists with his brother Charles at Oxford, 1730. Went out to Georgia as missionary, 1735. Returned to England, 1737, and in 1739 became associated with Whitfield in the organisation of the Methodist body. Travelled through all parts of the country, often preaching in the open air. Died in London, 1791, and buried in the City Road Chapel.

> "Probably no man ever exerted so great an influence on the religious condition of the people of England as John Wesley, and his influence has extended to the most remote parts of the world."

Sculptor unknown.

PLATE LXXXI.

BENJAMIN FRANKLIN, Philosopher, Politician and Philanthropist. Born at Boston, Massachusetts, U.S.A., 1706. Seventeenth son of Josiah Franklin, a tallow chandler. Bound apprentice to his uncle James, a printer, in 1716. Proceeded to Philadelphia, 1723, and established himself there as a bookseller, 1729. Became proprietor and editor of the "Pennsylvania Gazette" in the same year. First published his "Poor Richard's Almanack" in 1732. Elected Clerk of the Assembly of Pennsylvania, 1736; Postmaster of Philadelphia, 1737; and Deputy Postmaster-General of the British Colonies, 1753. Established the identity of lightning and electricity in 1749. Made several journeys to England as agent for Pennsylvania, and took an active part in the negotiations between the mother country and the colonies, which culminated in the Declaration of Independence being signed in 1776. As Commissioner for the United States he signed the Treaty of Independence at Paris, 1783. Died at Philadelphia, 1790.

> "He deemed nothing which concerned the interests or happiness of mankind as unworthy of his attention, and rarely, if ever, bestowed his attention on any subject without obtaining permanently useful results."

Painted at Paris by F. Baricolo, after a portrait by J. S. Duplessis, 1783.

PLATE LXXXII.

JOHN HOWARD, Philanthropist. Born at Hackney, about 1726. Son of a London tradesman. Set sail for Lisbon after the great earthquake, 1756. Married Sarah Loidore, 1741 ; Henrietta Croxton, 1758. Created High Sheriff of Bedfordshire, 1773, and began to devote himself to prison reform. Travelled through France and Germany visiting prisons and hospitals. Published his great work on prisons, 1777, which he dedicated to the House of Commons, and in 1789 brought out "An Account of the Principal Lazarettos in Europe." Proceeded to Turkey and Russia in 1790 to investigate the nature of the plague in the East. Caught infection from a fevered patient and died, and was buried at Kherson, in the South of Russia, 1790.

"The fame of Howard is peculiar. He is remembered not so much for his talents, as for that devotion to his suffering fellow-men in which he expended both his fortune and his life."

Painted by Mather Brown.

PLATE LXXXIII.

PRINCE CHARLES EDWARD STUART, known as "The Young Pretender." Son of Prince James Francis, called the "Old Pretender," and grandson of James II. Born at Rome, 1720, and educated at that city. Landed in Scotland, 1745, proclaimed his father King, and set up his standard at Edinburgh. Defeated Sir John Cope at Preston Pans, 1745, and having advanced as far as Derby, retreated to Scotland. Routed General Fawley at Falkirk, 1746, but was in turn utterly defeated by the Duke of Cumberland, at Culloden Moor, in the same year. Escaped after various adventures to St. Malo, and took up his residence in Rome under the title of "Count of Albany." Died at Frascati, 1788.

"On the whole, if Prince Charles had concluded his life soon after his miraculous escape, his character in history must have stood very high. As it was, his station is amongst those, a certain brilliant portion of whose life forms a remarkable contrast to all which precedes, and all which follows it."

Painted by Nicolas Largillièrre.

Plate LXXXIV.

THOMAS GAINSBOROUGH, R.A., Artist. Born at Sudbury, Suffolk, 1727. The youngest son of John Gainsborough, a clothier. His mother, a Miss Burroughs, excelled in painting flowers. From a very early age he drew from nature. When about ten years of age he was sent to the Grammar School at Sudbury. At the age of fifteen he was brought to London, where Gravelot gave him instruction in drawing. He worked in the Academy in St. Martin's Lane, and at Hayman's. Later he set up in Hatton Garden, and painted landscapes and small portraits. After an absence of four years he returned to his native place, and resumed there that study of nature which made him one of the greatest—if not the greatest—of English portrait painters. He married Miss Burr (1746), and removed to Ipswich, and later to Bath (1760). From this time he became "the fashion." He settled in London in 1774, and was one of the foundation members of the Royal Academy, but ceased to exhibit after 1784. He died in London, 1788, and was buried in Kew Churchyard, near his friend Joshua Kirby.

"Shortly before his death Gainsborough said to Sir Joshua Reynolds, 'We are all going to Heaven, and Van Dyck is of the company.' Truly this great English portrait painter has been exalted by his talents into the seventh heaven reserved for great, ennobling artists."

"The founder of the English School of landscape painting."

Painted by himself.

Plate LXXXV.

AUGUSTUS, VISCOUNT KEPPEL. Second son of William Anne Keppel, Earl of Albermarle. Born 1725. Educated at Westminster School. Entered the Navy, 1735. Served in the "Centurion" under Commodore Anson, 1740, in the celebrated voyage round the world. Commanded the squadron sent to co-operate with the troops in the reduction of Belle Island, 1761. Appointed Commodore and second in command, under Sir George Pocock, of the expedition against Havana, 1761, Created Rear-Admiral of the Blue, 1762. Raised to the peerage and appointed First Lord of the Admiralty, 1782. Died, 1786.

"In spite of almost overwhelming disadvantages, he achieved a brilliant reputation by the heroism, prudence, diligence, and humanity he displayed."

Painted by Sir Joshua Reynolds, P.R.A.

PLATE LXXXVI.

SIR WILLIAM BLACKSTONE, Legal Writer and Judge. Posthumous son of Charles Blackstone, of London. Born in Cheapside, London, 1723. Educated at Charterhouse and Pembroke College, Oxford, 1738. Entered at Middle Temple, 1741. Elected Fellow of All Souls, 1744. Took the degree of B.C.L., 1745. Called to the Bar, 1746. Appointed principal of New Inn Hall, 1761. M.P. for Hindon, 1761. Published his edition of the Great Charter and the Charter of the Forest, 1759. Married Sarah Clitherow, 1761. First volume of his "Commentaries" appeared, 1765. Made Justice of the Common Pleas, 1770. Died 1780, and was buried in the parish church of Wallingford.

"Lawyers turned to him to find for the first time English law made readable."

"It is still to Blackstone, in some form or other, that English law students turn who seek a general view of the subject."

Painted by Sir Joshua Reynolds, P.R.A.

PLATE LXXXVII.

CAPTAIN JAMES COOK, R.N., Navigator and Discoverer. Son of an agricultural labourer. Born at Marton, Yorkshire, 1728. Educated at the school of his native village. Apprenticed to Messrs. Walker, shipowners at Whitby, 1740. Joined the navy as able seaman on board the "Eagle," Captain Pallisser, 1755. Appointed master of the "Mercury," 1759, and of the "Northumberland," 1762. Married Miss Batts, 1762. Surveyed the Newfoundland island, 1763, and in 1768 commanded an astronomical expedition to the Pacific Ocean. Made a second voyage in 1772, during which he sailed upwards of 20,000 leagues. Set out on a search for the North West Passage, 1776. Discovered the Sandwich Islands, 1778, and lost his life in the following year at the hands of the natives of Hawaii.

"He was one of England's greatest navigators. A practical and scientific seaman; he was also a sagacious, self-possessed commander, kind although strict to his crew, and marked by indomitable perseverance and ready decision."

Painted by John Webber, R.A.

PLATE LXXXVIII.

DAVID GARRICK, Actor and Author. Born at Hereford, 1716. Son of an army captain. Educated at Lichfield Grammar School. Set out for London in company with Samuel Johnson, 1736. Adopted the stage as a profession, 1741. Made his *début* at Ipswich as Aboan, in "Oroonoko," and obtained a great success. Appeared in the same year as Richard III. at Goodman's Fields Theatre, London. Created great enthusiasm in Dublin, 1742. Became joint-patentee of Drury Lane, 1747. Visited Italy, 1763, and projected and conducted the jubilee at Stratford-on-Avon, 1769, in honour of Shakespeare. Died in London, 1779, and buried in Westminster Abbey.

"Garrick ranks as one of the very greatest—perhaps *the* very greatest of English actors. He exhibited a Shakespearian universality in the representation of character, and was equally at home in the highest flights of tragedy and the lowest depths of farce."

Painted by Robert Edge Pine.

PLATE LXXXIX.

OLIVER GOLDSMITH, Poet, Historian, Dramatist. Born at Pallas, County Longford, Ireland, 1728. His father was a poor curate, but by the benevolence of his uncle, Mr. Contarine, Oliver was enabled to enter the University of Dublin, 1744, where he took a B.A. degree, 1749. Having been a short time tutor in a family in Ireland, he determined to study medicine; and after nominally attending lectures in Edinburgh, he began those travels—for the most part on foot, and subsisting by the aid of his flute and the charity given to a poor scholar—which eventually led him to Leyden, through Holland, France, Germany and Switzerland, and even to Padua. He returned to England, 1756, and settled in London. He wrote obscurely for some time in periodicals of the day. "The Traveller" was published in 1764; "The Vicar of Wakefield," 1766; "The Good Natured Man," 1768; "The Deserted Village," 1770.

"She Stoops to Conquer" was acted in 1773. His improvidence kept him plunged in debt, and he died of a fever in the Temple, 1774, and was buried in the Temple Churchyard.

"In everything Goldsmith wrote, prose or verse, serious or comic, there is a peculiar delicacy and purity of sentiment, tinging, of course, the language and diction as well as the thought."

"He wrote like an angel, and spoke like poor Poll."

"Because Boswell could not appreciate the vivacity of the Irish temperament, that is no reason why we should regard Oliver Goldsmith as a half-inspired fool, who blundered into producing two of the most vital masterpieces in our language."

Painted by a pupil of Sir Joshua Reynolds.

Plate XC.

WILLIAM PITT, First Earl of Chatham, sometimes styled Pitt the Elder. Younger son of Robert Pitt, of Boconnoc, in Cornwall. Born, 1708. Educated at Eton and Oxford. Entered Parliament for Old Sarum, 1735. Became the leader of the "Patriots," and admitted to a subordinate place in the Broad Bottom Administration, 1742. In 1756 was nominally Secretary of State, but virtually Premier. He resigned in 1761 and remained out of office until 1766 when he received the royal command to form a ministry. He selected the almost sinecure office of Privy Seal with a seat in the House of Lords as Viscount Pitt and Earl of Chatham. He resigned in 1768, to hold office no more. He died two years later and was buried in Westminster Abbey.

"His oratory was of the most powerful kind. . . . . His upright and irreproachable character demanded the admiration of his enemies ; but his affectedness and haughtiness not unfrequently disgusted his friends, and pride rather than principle seems to have actuated his course at some important conjunctures of his life. He had, however, an intense love of country ; the grand object of his ambition being to make his native land safe against all contingencies."

Painted by Wm. Hoare, R.A.

Plate XCI.

WILLIAM HOGARTH, Artist. Born in London, 1697. Son of a Westmoreland schoolmaster. His inclination for art caused his father to apprentice him to a silver-plate engraver in Cranborne

Street, Liecester Fields. At the age of twenty-three he set up business for himself as an engraver, and obtained work as a book-illustrator. He made a run-away match with the daughter of Sir James Thornhill, the sergeant-painter, in 1729; was forgiven ultimately, and succeeded his father-in-law in 1757. In 1733 he removed to a house in Leicester Fields, where he lived for the rest of his life. He first obtained notoriety by his "Harlot's Progress," which was immediately followed by "The Rake's Progress," by the "Marriage à la mode," and by portraits. He published an "Analysis of Beauty," 1753. He died in 1764, and was buried at Chiswick.

"His graphic representations are indeed books; they have the teeming, fruitful, suggestive meaning of words. Other pictures we look at—his we read."

"No man was ever less a hero; you see him before you, and you fancy what he was—a jovial, honest, London citizen, stout and sturdy; a hearty, plain-spoken man, loving his laugh, his friend, his glass, his roast-beef of Old England."

Painted by himself in 1758.

PLATE XCII.

SAMUEL RICHARDSON, Novelist. Born in Derbyshire, 1689. Son of a joiner. After receiving a rustic education, he came to London, and was apprenticed to a printer named John Wilde, 1706. In the course of time he set up in business for himself, married Allington Wilde's daughter, and gradually rose to the highest place in his business. Was appointed first printer of the Journals of the House of Commons, and then, in 1754, Master of the Stationers' Company, and in 1760, became the purchaser of a half-share in the lucrative patent office of Printer to the King. Having acquired an easy fortune, he retired to North End, Fulham, where he passed an honourable old age in literary employment, surrounded by a little knot of female worshippers, whose adulatory incense his intense vanity made him greedily accept. His works are three in number, "Pamela," (1740); "Clarissa Harlowe," 1748, and "Sir Charles Grandison," 1753. He died in 1761, and was buried in St. Bride's, Fleet Street.

"Samuel Richardson must be regarded as the real founder of the romance of private life in English literature."

Painted by Joseph Highmore.

PLATE XCIII.

MARGARET ("PEG") WOFFINGTON, Actress. Born in Dublin of Irish parents, 1720. At eight years of age appeared as Captain Macheath in Madame Violante's Lilliputian Company. First appeared in London in 1740, at Covent Garden, as Sylvia in the "Recruiting Officer." Revisited Dublin with Garrick, 1742. She excelled in male characters and in higher comedy. Struck with paralysis, whilst speaking the epilogue to "As you like it," 1757, and died, 1760. Buried at Teddington.

"In a time of unusually beautiful women, she was one of the handsomest, and at the same time, least vain of any. Her great charm was her naturalness, and whatever the character she had to represent, she never failed to entirely identify herself with it."

Painted by Arthur Pond, about 1758.

PLATE XCIV.

GEORGE FREDERICK HANDEL, Composer. Born at Halle, Lower Saxony, 1685. Son of a surgeon, who was sixty-three when this son was born. He became a pupil of Zachau. His first opera, "Almira," was produced at Hamburg, 1705. He came to England, 1710. "Rinaldo" was produced in 1711. He was appointed Kapelmeister to the Elector of Hanover who, shortly after, succeeded to the English throne. His operatic speculations in the Haymarket having failed in 1734, Handel turned his attention to sacred music. "Esther" was the first of his nineteen English oratorios. "Saul" and "Israel in Egypt" were composed in 1738, "The Messiah" and "Samson," 1741; "Judas Maccabeus, 1746; "Solomon," 1748; "Jephtha," 1751. He also wrote thirty-nine Italian operas, ninty-four cantatas, and about two hundred other works in various departments of musical expression. It is, however, an undeniable fact that, besides repeating himself, he drew largely and unhesitatingly on the resources of his predecessors and contemporaries. "The Harmonious Blacksmith" was the composition of Wagensil or of some older and less known composer. Handel never married. He died in Brook Street, 1759, and was buried in Westminster Abbey.

"Handel left behind him in his adopted country a name and a popularity which never has been, and probably never will be, rivalled by that of any other composer."

A bust by Roubillac.

PLATE XCV.

JAMES WOLFE, General. Son of Lieut.-Colonel Wolfe, was born at Westerham, Kent, 1726. Received his commission as ensign, 1742. Took part in the battle of Dettingen, 1743. Distinguished himself by his conduct at Lanfeldt, 1747. Appointed Major of the 20th Foot, 1749. Joined Boscawen and Amherst in the reduction of Louisberg, 1758. Advanced to the rank of Major-General, and set out on an expedition to Quebec, 1758. After a gallant contest, the French were routed and Montcalm, their commander, killed. Wolfe expired on the field of battle, and his body was brought to England and interred at Greenwich.

"But that he had the true genius for command, which needed only time and further opportunity to win for him a fame still more splendid, it is scarcely permitted us to doubt."

Painted by J. S. C. Schaak.

PLATE XCVI.

REV. ISAAC WATTS, D.D., Nonconformist Divine and Hymn Writer. Born at Southampton, 1674. Author of the "Divine and Moral Songs for Children." He died in 1748, and was buried in Bunhill fields.

"This childless saint and scholar assured the perpetuity of his name by his 'Divine Songs,' which, in spite of many a metrical defect and much hopeless prose, show strength, sanity, and the right simplicity without weakness."

Painted by Sir Godfrey Kneller.

PLATE XCVII.

JONATHAN SWIFT, D.D., Divine, Satirist, Author. Born at Dublin, 1667, of English family and descent. Educated at a school at Kilkenny, entered Trinity College, Dublin, 1682. Entered the household of Sir William Temple, 1688. Having entered into holy orders, he went to Ireland as chaplain to Earl Berkeley and received the living of Laracor and Rathbeggan. He lived at Laracor until 1710. Made Dean of St. Patrick's, 1713. From 1714 to 1720 he resided mostly in Ireland. The death of Stella happened in 1728. In 1741 he was afflicted with a painful inflammation which gradually merged into a state of idiocy that lasted until his death in

1745. He was buried in his own cathedral of St. Patrick's. He published the pasquinade, "The Tale of a Tub," 1704; The Seven Famous Letters signed M. B. Drapier, 1724; "The Travels of Gulliver," 1726. These, his "Journal to Stella," and innumerable pamphlets and historical and political tracts, all exhibit the vigour of his reasoning, the admirable force and directness of his style and his unscrupulous ferocity of invention.

"We laugh with Rabelais, we sneer with Voltaire; with Swift we despise and abhor. He will notably be ever regarded as one of the greatest masters of English prose, but his poetical works will give him a prominent place among the writers of his age."

In his epitaph he speaks of resting "ubi sæva indignatio ulterius cor lacerare nequit."

Painted by Charles Jervas.

PLATE XCVIII.

ALEXANDER POPE, Poet. Born in London, 1688, son of a linen-draper in Lombard Street. Educated at Twyford, near Winchester, and Mr. Deane's school near Hyde Park Corner. The boy was of almost dwarfish stature, but like many other deformed and dwarfish persons he possessed a singularly intellectual and expressive countenance. He exhibited an extraordinary precocity of intellect. At sixteen he commenced his literary career by composing a collection of "Pastorals." His translations from "Statius" were published in 1712; "Essay on Criticism," 1711; "Windsor Forest," 1713; the mock-heroic poem, "The Rape of the Lock," 1714; "The Temple of Fame" and "January and May" followed, and about this time he undertook the laborious enterprise of translating into English verse the Iliad and the Odyssey. The first volume appeared, 1715, and the Iliad was completed in 1720. The satire, "Dunciad," appeared in 1728-29—to be added to in 1742 and 1743, and the "Essay on Man," 1734. His "Epistles" were written between 1731 and 1735. He died 1744 and was buried at Twickenham.

"Unquestionably the most illustrous writer of his age, hardly if at all inferior to Swift in the vigour, the perfection, and the originality of his genius."

Drawn in crayons and attributed to William Hoare, of Bath.

PLATE XCIX.

HON. ROGER NORTH, Lawyer, Historian and Biographer. Son of Dudley, fourth Lord North, and nephew of the first Earl of Manchester. Born at Tostock, in Suffolk, 1653. Educated at Thetford School and Jesus College, Cambridge. Admitted at the Inner Temple, 1669. Became Steward of the Courts to Archbishop Sheldon, and was appointed King's Counsel, 1682, and Solicitor-General to the Duke of York, 1684. Published "Examen," 1740; "The Lives of the Norths," 1742, and an "Essay on Music." Died at Rougham, 1734.

Painted by Sir Peter Lely, 1680.

PLATE C.

SIR RICHARD STEELE, Author. Born at Dublin, of English parents, 1672. Educated at the Charterhouse, where he was a school-fellow of Addison, and Merton College, Oxford. Enlisted as a private in the Horse Guards. He wrote a religious treatise entitled "The Christian Hero," and his first successful comedy, "The Funeral," or "Grief à la Mode," was produced in 1701. In 1709 he founded "The Tatler," which was remodelled into the celebrated "Spectator," 1711, and followed by "The Guardian," 1713. He plunged into politics, was elected for Stockbridge, but expelled for his political writings. On the accession of the House of Hanover, however, he was again admitted to Parliament as M.P. for Boroughbridge, and appointed surveyor to the Royal Stables at Hampton Court. He was knighted in 1715, but after dissipating more than one fortune, he died in poverty at Carmarthen, and was buried in St. Peter's Church, 1729.

" He was a man of ready, though not solid talents, writing with ease, pleasantry and knowledge of life."

Painted in 1712 by Jonathan Richardson.

PLATE CI.

SIR ISAAC NEWTON, F.R.S., Philosopher. Born at Woolsthorpe, Lincolnshire, 1642. Educated at Grantham Grammar School and Trinity College, Cambridge. Discovered the nature of light and colours, 1664, and the law of universal gravitation, 1665. Elected Fellow of the Royal Society, 1671; M.P. for Cambridge

University, 1672; and procured a seat in the Convention Parliament in 1689. Appointed Warden of the Mint, 1696, and Master of the Mint, 1699. Elected M.P. for his University, 1701. Created President of the Royal Society, 1703. Knighted, 1705. Published his "Principia," 1687, and his "Observations on the Prophecies" appeared in 1733. Died 1727, and was buried in Westminster Abbey.

"The most remarkable mathematician and natural philosopher of his own, or perhaps of any other age."

Painted by John Vanderbank.

PLATE CII.

SIR CHRISTOPHER WREN, F.R.S., Architect and Mathematician. Son of Dr. Christopher Wren, Dean of Windsor, Chaplain to Charles I., and Registrar of the Order of the Garter. Born at Knoyle, Wiltshire, 1632. Educated at Westminster School, under Dr. Busby, and at Wadham College, Oxford. Became Professor of Astronomy at Gresham College, 1657. Returned to Oxford as Savilian Professor of Astronomy, 1661. Created D.C.L. in the same year. Was one of the original founders of the Royal Society. Visited Paris, 1665. Chosen to be the architect of the new St. Paul's Cathedral, 1675, the last and highest stone of which was laid in 1710. Besides more than fifty churches, he built the Royal Exchange, 1667; Customs House, 1668; Temple Bar, 1670; Monument, 1671-77; College of Physicians, 1674-98; Royal Observatory, Greenwich, 1675; Chelsea Hospital, 1682-90; Hampton Court, 1690; Greenwich Hospital, 1696; Marlborough House, 1709; the towers at the West Front of Westminster Abbey, 1713. Knighted in 1672. Elected President of the Royal Society, 1680, and M.P. for New Windsor, 1689. Died in 1723, and was buried in St. Paul's Cathedral.

"Steele, in the 'Tatler,' introduces Wren in the character of Nestor, and few have been found since that time hardy enough to call in question the well-merited reputation of Sir Christopher Wren, as a distinguished architect, mathematician, and scientific observer."

Painted by Sir Godfrey Kneller.

PLATE CIII.

RIGHT HON. JOSEPH ADDISON, Poet, Statesman and Essayist. Born in Wiltshire, 1672. Son of Lancelot Addison, Dean of Lichfield. Educated at Charterhouse, and Queen's and Magdalen Colleges, Oxford, where he distinguished himself for his exquisite taste in Latin verse. His knowledge of the Roman literature was profound. Travelled abroad under the patronage of Lord Halifax. Wrote "The Campaign," 1704. Henceforward his career was brilliant and successful. The opera "Rosamund" appeared 1707; the tragedy of "Cato," 1713; and numerous prose and poetical contributions to Steele's group of publications occupied a well-filled life. He was appointed secretary to the Marquess of Wharton in Ireland, 1709, and elected M.P. for Malmesbury; Secretary to the Lords Justices, 1714, and made Secretary of State, 1717. He married the Dowager Countess of Warwick, 1716. He died at Holland House, 1719, and was buried in Westminster Abbey.

"The immense fertility of invention displayed in his essays, the variety of their subjects, and the simpler felicity of their treatment, will ever place them among the masterpieces of fiction and of criticism."

"For graceful style, for polished satire, for delicate delineation of character, Addison has never been surpassed."

Painted in 1719 by Michael Dahl.

PLATE CIV.

GILBERT BURNET, D.D., Bishop of Salisbury, Historian. Son of Robert Burnet, an advocate. Born at Edinburgh, 1643, and educated at the Marischal College, Aberdeen. Ordained, 1665, and officiated for five years as minister of Saltoun, East Lothian. Appointed Professor of Divinity at Glasgow, 1669. Removed to the Rolls Chapel, in London, 1675. Retired to the continent, 1685. Returned to England as chaplain to William, Prince of Orange, 1688, and was shortly afterwards appointed Bishop of Salisbury. Published "Memoirs of the Dukes of Hamilton," 1676; "History of the Reformation," 1679-1714; and his "Exposition of the Thirty-nine Articles," 1699. Died in London, 1715, and was buried in St. James's Church, Clerkenwell.

"He was a man of strict, almost of puritanical virtue; yet his charity, geniality, and moderation of sentiment might be imitated with advantage even in our own day. His style is neither elegant nor correct, yet the honesty, earnestness, simplicity, and vigour of his writings, as well as their fulness of details, make his works very valuable to the student of history."

Painted by John Riley, in 1690.

PLATE CV.

THOMAS BETTERTON, Actor and Dramatist. Was born in Westminster, 1635. Apprenticed by his father, a cook in the service of Charles I., to a bookseller at Charing Cross. First appeared at the Cockpit Theatre, Drury Lane, and in 1661 joined the "Duke's Company," organized by Sir William Davenant in Lincoln's Inn Fields. His best known plays are: "The Roman Virgin," "The Prophetess," "The Amorous Widow," and "The Bondman, or Love and Liberty." Until the time of Garrick, the most versatile and perfect actor on the English stage. He was gifted with a handsome person and melodious voice. Died, 1710, and was buried in Westminster Abbey.

"Betterton was an actor as Shakespeare was an author, both without competitors."

Painted by Sir Godfrey Kneller.

PLATE CVI.

BARBARA VILLIERS, DUCHESS OF CLEVELAND. Only daughter of William, Viscount Grandison. Born, 1640. Married Roger Palmer, afterwards Earl of Castlemain. Created Duchess of Cleveland by Charles II., and became mother of the Duke of Southampton and of the Duke of Grafton. One of the celebrated beauties of the Court of Charles II. Died, 1709.

"The splendid termagant."

Copied from Sir Peter Lely.

CVII.

CATHERINE OF BRAGANZA. Daughter of John IV., King of Portugal. Born at the Palace Villa Viçosa, Portugal, 1638. Married to Charles II., 1662, thereby bringing to England the possession of Bombay and Tangier. After the king's death, she resided at Somerset House, and also at Hammersmith. Returned to Portugal, 1692, and afterwards acted as regent to her brother, Pedro II. Died, 1705. Buried at Belem, Portugal.

"And all her people say of her to be a very fine and handsome lady, and very discreet."

Painted by Dirk Stoop.

PLATE CVIII.

TITUS OATES, *alias* Ambrose. Son of the rector of Marsham, who became an Anabaptist preacher. Born at Oakham, 1649. Educated at Merchant Taylors' School and Caius College, Cambridge. Was in turn an Anabaptist minister, clergyman of the Church of England and Roman Catholic. Came forward as discoverer of a supposed Popish plot against the King, 1677, and on his evidence many eminent Catholics suffered death. Received a handsome pension and a residence in Whitehall for his services. Tried before the Court of King's Bench, 1685, convicted of perjury, and sentenced to be whipped, pilloried, and imprisoned for life. Released under William III. in 1688, and again pensioned. Died in 1705.

"He, as a mere vagabond adventurer, set himself to live by his wits, in the evil exercise of which he devised the atrocious scheme with which his name is identified in history."

Drawn and engraved from the life by Robert White.

PLATE CIX.

JOHN LOCKE, Philosopher. Born at Wrington, near Bristol, 1632, son of a lawyer. Educated at Westminster and Christ Church, Oxford, where he took his M.A. in 1658. He travelled much abroad. He attached himself to Lord Ashley, afterwards Earl of Shaftesbury, and was nominated in 1672 Secretary of the Presentations. Upon the fall of his patron he retreated to Holland, but returned in the same fleet which conveyed Queen Mary, 1688, and was employed in the public service. His "Letters on Toleration" were published, 1689, and his greatest and most universally known work, the "Essay on the Human Understanding," the next year. He was the friend of Newton, and the founder in England of modern metaphysical inquiry. He died in 1704 and is buried at High Laver.

"The champion of intellectual liberty, vindicating the rights of reason in politics and in religion."

Painted by T. Brownover.

PLATE CX.

SAMUEL PEPYS, P.R.S., the Diarist. Born, 1633, the friendless cadet of an ancient family. After receiving some education at Huntingdon, St. Paul's, and the University of Cambridge, is supposed to have for some time exercised the trade of a tailor. He obtained his first appointment in Government service through the influence of Sir Edward Montagu, and was Secretary to the Navy Board during the reign of Charles II. and James II. President of the Royal Society 1684 and 1685. His Diary, upon which his fame rests, was written for his own use in cypher and covers the eleven years 1659-69, but was not deciphered and published until 1825. He died in 1703, and was buried at St. Olave's, Hart Street.

"Pepys was notably by nature a thorough gossip, curious as an old woman, with a strong taste for occasional jollifications, and a touch of the antiquary and curiosity-hunter; but he was necessarily brought into contact with all classes of persons, from the King and his Ministers down to the poor half-starved sailors, whose pay he had to distribute."

"An original and even comic personality."

Painted at the age of 34 by John Hayls.

PLATE CXI.

KING WILLIAM III. Born, 1650. Grandson of Charles I. and son of William II., Prince of Orange. Stadtholder of Holland, K.G., 1653. Married Mary, daughter of King James II., 1677. Landed at Torbay, November, 1688, and in February, 1689, conjointly with his wife, accepted the sovereignty of Great Britain and Ireland, Died, 1702.

"Had mortal action e'er a nobler scope?
 The hero comes to liberate, not defy;
And, while he marches on with righteous hope,
 Conqueror behold! expected anxiously.
The vacillating bondman of the Pope
 Shrinks from the verdict of his steadfast eye.

Painted by Jan Wyck.

PLATE CXII.

JOHN DRYDEN, Poet and Dramatist. Born in Northamptonshire, 1631. Grandson of Sir Erasmus Dryden, Bart. Educated under Dr. Busby at Westminster, and at Trinity College, Cambridge, where he took his B.A., 1654. At the Restoration he attached himself to the Royalist party. His whole life is filled with vigorous and unremitting literary labours, and presents but few events unconnected with the successive composition of his works. "Astræa Redux" appeared, 1660; "Annus Mirabilis," 1667; his "Essay on Dramatic Poetry," about 1668; "Absalom and Achitophel," 1681; the satire "Mac-Flecknoe," 1682; "The Hind and the Panther," 1687; "Alexander's Feast," 1697; his "Fables," 1700. Was made Poet Laureate, 1670. His dramatic career began about 1662, and his work for the stage constitutes a very large portion of his entire compositions. He married Lady Elizabeth Howard in 1663. Died in 1700, and was buried in Westminster Abbey.

"Dryden must be regarded as the first enlightened critic who appeared in the English language."

"And Dryden in immortal strain
Had raised the Table Round again,
But that a ribald King and Court
Bade him toil on to make them sport."

Painted by Sir Godfrey Kneller.

PLATE CXIII.

THE SEVEN BISHOPS who were committed to the Tower, 1688, for refusing to distribute the King's Declaration of Indulgence for liberty of conscience, were as follows: William Sancroft, Archbishop of Canterbury; Thomas Ken, Bishop of Bath and Wells; John Lake, Bishop of Chichester; William Lloyd, Bishop of St. Asaph; Jonathan Trelawnay, Bishop of Bristol; Francis Turner, Bishop of Ely; Thomas White, Bishop of Peterborough. After a trial in the Court of Queen's Bench, they were acquitted and set at liberty.

Painter unknown.

PLATE CXIV.

ELEANOR ("NELL") GWYN, Actress. Born of Welsh parents at Hereford, 1650. First known in London as an orange girl in the pit of the Royal Theatre. Made her first appearance on the stage in 1665. Scored her chief successes as Desdemona and Ophelia, and in the recitation of epilogues, several of which were specially composed for her by Dryden. Retired from the stage, 1671, and presented with luxurious apartments at Whitehall by Charles II. Was chiefly instrumental in the foundation of Chelsea Hospital. Died, 1687, and was buried at St. Martin's-in-the-Fields.

"In her character she was frank, unsentimental, and English; as an actress she excelled in comedy, captivating her audience with her gay, saucy, and sprightly manner."

Painted by Sir Peter Lely.

PLATE CXV.

JAMES SCOTT, DUKE OF MONMOUTH, K.G. Born at Rotterdam, 1649. An illegitimate son of Charles II. by Lucy Walters. Known when young as "Captain Crofts." Created Duke of Monmouth, 1663, and made Master of the Horse, 1665. Married Anne, daughter and heiress of Francis, Duke of Buccleuch, 1665. He was created Duke of Buccleuch, Lord Great Chamberlain and High Admiral of Scotland. The collapse of his rebellion at the Battle of Sedgmoor, 1685, caused him to end his life on Tower Hill, 15th June of the same year.

"He had several good qualities in him, and some that were as bad. He was soft and gentle even to excess, and too easy to those who had credit with him. He was both sincere and good-natured, and understood war well. But he was too much given to pleasure and to favourites."

Painted by William Wissing.

PLATE CXVI.

CHARLES II. Son of Charles I. and Henrietta Maria of France. Born 1630. Upon the execution of his father, in 1649, he was proclaimed king by the Scots. He met and was defeated by Cromwell at Worcester, 1649, and escaped to France. He returned to London in triumph, 1660. He married Catherine of Braganza, 1662. In 1666, the Great Plague and Fire of London occurred. After a long succession of drawn engagements he made peace with the Dutch in 1674. Viscount Stafford was murdered in 1679. Charles II. died from a fit of apoplexy at Whitehall, 1685.

"Whatever were the personal failings or vices of the king, he never forfeited the love of his subjects."

"Crime succeeded to crime, and disgrace to disgrace, till the race accursed of God and man was a second time driven forth, to wander on the face of the earth, and to be a byword and a shaking of the head to the nations."

Painted by Mrs. Beale.

Plate CXVII.

PRINCE RUPERT, K.G. Son of Frederick V., Count Palatine of the Rhine, and Elizabeth, daughter of James I. Born at Prague, 1619. Received a commission from his uncle, Charles I., to command a regiment of horse at Worcester against the Parliamentarians. His impetuosity proved fatal to the Royalist cause at Marston Moor, 1644. His conduct at Naseby, 1645, and his hasty surrender at Bristol estranged him from the king. Recalled, 1648, and appointed to the command of the royal fleet. Defeated by Admiral Blake, 1650, and escaped to the West Indies. Served with distinction under the Duke of York after the Restoration, 1660. Improved the mechanical mode of engraving in mezzotint. Died in Spring Gardens, 1682, and was buried in Westminster Abbey.

"The impetuosity which he displayed in battle would have proved of greater value to the royalists, had it not been for his rashness and petulant disregard of orders."

Painted by Sir Peter Lely.

Plate CXVIII.

SAMUEL BUTLER, Author. Born at Strensham, Worcestershire, 1612. Son of a farmer. Educated at the Cathedral School, Worcester. He performed the office of clerk to Jeffries, a country J.P. Afterwards he entered the house of Elizabeth, Countess of Kent, and probably that of Sir Samuel Luke, a wealthy and popular county magnate, also. It is said that Luke himself was the original of Butler's inimitable caricature of Hudibras. At the Restoration, Butler became secretary to the Earl of Carberry. About this time he married Mrs. Herbert, a lady of birth and fortune. The fortune was not properly secured, however, and Butler died in extreme poverty at his lodging in Rose Street, Covent Garden, and was buried in the churchyard of St. Paul's in that neighbourhood, 1680. His great work, the famous satire of "Hudibras," was published at irregular intervals, the first part in 1663, the second in the following year, and the third in 1678. He also composed a mass of miscellaneous writings.

"Butler is at once intensely concise and abundantly rich. His expressions, taken singly, have the pregnant brevity of proverbs; while the fertility of his illustrations is perpetually opening new vistas of comic and witty associations."

Drawn in crayons by E. Lutterel.

PLATE CXIX.

MARY DAVIS, Dancer and Actress. Was one of the four leading women in Sir William Davenant's "Duke's Company" at Lincoln's Inn Fields, between the years 1664 and 1668. Her daughter, by King Charles II., was the mother of James, Earl of Derwentwater, who was executed on Tower Hill, 1716. Died in 1678.

". . . . . . delight of all the nobler sort.
Pride of the stage, and darling of the Court."

Painted by Sir Peter Lely.

PLATE CXX.

ANDREW MARVEL, Poet and Satirist. Born, 1621. Son of a minister and schoolmaster, at Kingston-upon-Hull. Entered at Trinity College, Cambridge, 1633. He was attached to the English Embassy at Constantinople, afterwards gave instruction in the family of Fairfax. He became, in 1657, assistant to Milton, who was then Latin secretary. At the Restoration he was elected M.P. for Hull. The King took great pleasure in his conversation although he is said not to have been eloquent. He took an active part in the controversies of the day. He died in 1678 and was buried in the church of St. Giles's in the Fields. He deserves an honourable place among the minor poets of his day.

"His 'Thoughts in a Garden' are full of sweet and pleasant fancies, and exhibit a great delicacy of expression, often exquisite from its very quaintness. In his satirical verses on the Dutch he has a droll exaggeration and ingenious buffoonery; many of the ideas are worthy of the quaint and learned fancy of Butler."

Painter unknown.

PLATE CXXI.

EDWARD COCKER, Arithmetician. Born, 1631. His name became proverbial for exactness and precision, and it is no mean testimony to his fame that "according to Cocker," has passed down to our day as a common saying. His "Arithmetick" was published, after his death, in 1678, and went through many editions, long remaining the standard work on the subject. He compiled an English dictionary and published a book of sentences for writing known as "Cocker's Morals." He also engraved on silver many copy books for handwriting. Died, 1675, and buried at St. George's, Southwark.

Painter uncertain.

PLATE CXXII.

EDWARD HYDE, First Earl of CLARENDON, Historian and Lord Chancellor. Born at Dinton, in Wiltshire, 1608. Educated at Magdalen Hall, Oxford. Entered at the Middle Temple, but soon abandoned the bar for political life. Represented Wootton Bassett in the Short Parliament of 1640, and was a conspicuous orator in the "Long." After a violent quarrel with Hampden he passed over to the Royalist side, and when the King arrived at York, 1642, he fled to him from Westminster. He was knighted during the Parliament held at Oxford and appointed Chancellor of the Exchequer. During the Republic and Protectorate he remained abroad. At the Restoration he was installed Chancellor, made first a Baron, and afterwards, in 1661, Earl of Clarendon. Through the marriage of his daughter to the Duke of York he became grandfather to the Queens of England, Mary and Anne. He accumulated great wealth, but was impeached for high treason, was banished, and during his exile in France completed his celebrated "History of the Great Rebellion," and an account of his own life. He died at Rouen, 1674, and was buried in Westminster Abbey.

"Not only was he an actor in the political drama of that momentous epoch, but he holds an honourable place among English historians by means of his history of the events in which he had taken part."

Drawn and engraved from life by David Loggan.

PLATE CXXIII.

JOHN MILTON, Poet and Statesman. Born in Bread Street, London, 1608. Son of a money-scrivener. Educated at St. Paul's School and Christ College, Cambridge. He left Cambridge, 1632, after taking his M.A. He travelled on the Continent and had an interview with Galileo, "then grown old, a prisoner of the Inquisition." He returned, and opened a school in 1640. In 1649 he was appointed Latin Secretary to the Council of State. The loss of his sight became total in 1662. His eyes, even from early youth, had been delicate. He married Mary, eldest daughter of Richard Powell, J.P., 1643; Catherine Woodcock, 1656; and Elizabeth Minshull, 1663. He died at his house in Bunhill Fields, 1674, and was buried in the Chancel of St. Giles's, Cripplegate. His first attempts in poetry were made as early as his thirteenth year, and his "Hymn on the Nativity" was written, as a college exercise, in his 21st year. The pastoral drama, or masque, of

"Comus," appeared in 1634, and "Lycidas," "L'Allegro," and "Il Penseroso" belong to this period also. The "Areopagitica," in defence of the liberty of the press, and his curious "Tractate of Education" were published in 1644. About this time he began his "History of England." Numerous controversial treatises, historical, political and religious, followed. He finished the great epic, "Paradise Lost," 1665, and "Paradise Regained" and the noble and pathetic tragedy of "Samson Agonistes" are attributed to 1670.

"John Milton, the poet, the statesman, the philosopher, the glory of English literature, the champion and martyr of English liberty."

"There is no spectacle in the history of literature more touching and sublime than Milton, blind, poor, persecuted, and alone, 'Fallen upon evil days and evil tongues, with dangers and with darkness compassed round,' retiring into obscurity to compose those immortal epics which have placed him among the greatest poets of all time."

Painted by Pieter van der Plaas.

PLATE CXXIV.

HENRIETTA MARIA, Queen Consort of Charles I. Daughter of Henry IV. of France. Born at the Louvre, 1609. Married Charles I., 1625. Impeached by the Commons, 1643. Quitted England in 1644, and returned on the restoration of the Monarchy, 1660. Died at Colombes, near Paris, 1669, and buried in the church of St. Denis.

"Light-hearted, joyous and innocent, but apparently incapable of sustained application when her husband's troubles began."

Painted in the school of Van Dyck.

PLATE CXXV.

WILLIAM HARVEY, M.D. The discoverer of the circulation of the blood. Son of a yeoman. Born at Folkestone, Kent, 1578. Educated at Canterbury Grammar School, and Caius College, Cambridge. Proceeded to the University of Padua, where he studied under Fabricius de Aquapendente, and took his degree of M.D., 1602. Appointed physician to St. Bartholomew's Hospital,

1609, and, in 1615, Lumleian lecturer at the College of Physicians. He first published his "Theory of the Circulation of the Blood" in 1628. Created physician-extraordinary to James I., 1618, and formally chosen physician to Charles I., 1632. Was present with the king at the battle of Edgehill, 1642, and was elected warden of Merton College, 1645. Appointed president of the College of Physicians, 1654, but declined the office. Died in London, 1657, and was buried at Hempstead, in Essex.

"His discovery remains to-day the greatest in the history of physiology, and its whole honour belongs to Harvey."

Painter unknown.

Plate CXXVI.

INIGO JONES, Architect. Born near Smithfield, 1573. Son of a clothworker. Visited Italy and painted landscapes. Practised as an architect at Copenhagen under the patronage of King Christian IV. On returning to London he was attached to the service of Henry, Prince of Wales. Constructed with Ben Jonson many of the Court masques. Was appointed Surveyor of Works to the Crown, 1615. He completed the Banqueting House, Whitehall, 1622. He added a classic portico to old St. Paul's Cathedral, built the Queen's House at Greenwich, and laid out Lincoln's Inn Fields and Covent Garden Market. He built many noblemen's houses throughout the country. He was not married. Died at Somerset House, 1652, and was buried at St. Benet's, Paul's Wharf.

Copied by Old Stone from Van Dyck.

Plate CXXVII.

HENRY IRETON, one of Cromwell's generals, and his son-in-law. Born at Attenborough, Nottinghamshire, 1611. Educated at Trinity College, Oxford. Joined the Parliamentary forces, 1642. Distinguished himself at the battle of Naseby, 1645, and married Bridget, eldest daughter of Oliver Cromwell, 1646. Became Lord Deputy of Ireland and died at Limerick, 1651. His body was buried in Westminster Abbey, but disinterred at the Restoration, 1660, and hung on the gibbet at Tyburn.

"A man of melancholic, reserved, dark nature, who communicated his thoughts to very few, so that for the most part he resolved alone, but was never diverted from any resolution he had taken."

Painted by Robert Walker.

Plate CXXVIII.

KING CHARLES I. Born at Dunfermline, 1600. Son of James I. and Anne of Denmark. Succeeded to the throne in 1625. Married Henrietta Maria, youngest daughter of Henri IV. of France. Civil War between the King and the Parliamentary forces broke out in 1642, the drawn battle of Edgehill being fought on October 23 of this year. Prince Rupert was defeated at Marston Moor by Oliver Cromwell, and the last battle (which decided the fate of Charles) was fought at Naseby, in Northamptonshire. Charles gave himself up to the Scottish army who eventually sold him to the Parliament for the sum of £400,000, the arrears of their pay due from Parliament. Cromwell as head of the Independents, caused Charles to be seized and conveyed finally to Windsor. He was brought to trial for high treason, condemned, and beheaded at Whitehall, January 30, 1649.

"He had, in truth, none who loved him, till his misfortunes softened his temper, and excited sympathy."

"His death crowned the crimes of the rebellion, and with him died, for a time, the liberties of Englishmen."

"Few personages in history have had so much of their actions revealed and commented upon as Charles; it is, perhaps, a mortifying truth that those who have stood highest with posterity have seldom been those who have been most accurately known."

Painted (probably by Old Stone) after Van Dyck.

Plate CXXIX.

WILLIAM LAUD, Archbishop of Canterbury. Son of a clothier. Born at Reading, 1573. Educated at Reading Grammar School and St. John's College, Oxford; became a Fellow in 1593, and took his degree of M.A. in 1598. Ordained in 1601, and preferred to the vicarage of Stanford, Northamptonshire, 1607. Appointed Rector of Tilbury, 1609; President of St. John's College, 1611; Prebendary of Lincoln, 1614; and Archdeacon of Huntingdon, 1615. Consecrated Bishop of St. David's, 1621, and translated to the See of Bath and Wells, 1625. In 1628 he was made Bishop of London. Held supreme position in the High-Commission and Star-Chamber Courts. Became Archbishop of Canterbury and

Chancellor of Dublin University, 1633. Impeached by the Commons and committed to the Tower, 1640. Brought to trial on a charge of treason, 1643, and executed on Tower Hill, 1645, buried in the Chapel St. John's College, 1663.

"The Church of England was gradually penetrated with his spirit, and the high value which she has come to put on religious ceremonies is partly owing to the pertinacious efforts of the archbishop."

Copied by Henry Stone from the original picture by Van Dyck.

PLATE CXXX.

JOHN HAMPDEN, Patriot. Born in London, 1594. Son of William Hampden, of Hampden, Bucks, and first cousin of Oliver Cromwell. Entered as a gentleman commoner at Magdalen College, Oxford, 1609. Admitted to the Inner Temple, 1613. Entered the House of Commons as member for Grampound, 1621, Sat for Wendover in the first three Parliaments of Charles I. Prosecuted before the Court of the Exchequer, 1637, for resistance to the imposition of ship-money. Elected for Wendover and Buckingham County in the Long Parliament, 1640. He was one of the five members whom Charles attempted to seize in the House, 1642. Raised and became colonel of a regiment in the Parliamentary Army under the Earl of Essex. Died in 1643, of a wound received at Chalgrove Field, Oxfordshire, during an engagement with Prince Rupert, and buried in the Church of Great Hampden.

"The great leader in the fight for freedom—a man to whom the one pound eleven and sixpence, at which he was assessed, was of no consequence, but to whom the arbitrary exaction of the odd sixpence was of very great consequence indeed."

Sculptor unknown.

PLATE CXXXI.

SIR JOHN SUCKLING, Poet and Courtier. Born at Whitton, Middlesex, 1609. His father, also a knight, held office as Secretary of State and Controller of the Household at the Court of James I. Educated at Trinity College, Cambridge. Served in Germany under Gustavus Adolphus. Returned to England, 1632, and joined in an attempt to rescue Strafford from the Tower. He was one of the first professed admirers of Shakespeare. His works consist of a prose treatise, entitled "An Account of Religion by Reason," a collection of "Letters," and a series of miscellaneous poems, beginning with "A Session of the Poets," published in 1637. Died at Paris, 1642, buried in the cemetery attached to the Protestant Church there.

"The fame of Suckling rests on his songs and ballads, which are inimitable for their ease, gaiety, and pure poetic diction. A few pages of amatory lyrics have embalmed his name for all posterity."

Painted by Theodore Russell, after Van Dyck.

PLATE CXXXII.

BEN JONSON, Poet and Playwright. Born in Westminster, 1573. Educated at the parish school of St. Martin's and at Westminster, to which school he went through the assistance of William Camden, then one of the masters. In his youth he followed for a little the trade of his step-father (a bricklayer), then went to fight in the Low Countries, and then followed the bent of his genius by joining the players. He was not successful on the stage, left it and wrote Masques for the Court, but fell out with Inigo Jones, who supplied the machinery, and lost favour with the Court. Became Poet Laureate in 1619 and received the honorary degree of Master of Arts from Oxford University. He died in 1637 and was buried in Westminster Abbey. His first comedy, "Every Man in his Humour," was produced, 1598; "Every Man out of his Humour, 1599; "Cynthia's Revels," 1600; "The Poetaster," 1601; "Sejanus," 1603; "Volpone," 1605; "The Silent Woman," 1609; "The Alchemist," 1610; "Catiline," 1611.

"Like Milton, Ben Jonson has a mind so highly cultivated that turns of thought or expression give evidence of his scholarship in every page he writes. The spark of scholarship so flashed into the native humour of the poet is anything but pedantry. It is a finer light in light, wit within wit."

"O rare Ben Jonson."

An old copy from Gerard Honthorst.

PLATE CXXXIII.

CHILDREN OF KING CHARLES I., WITH A LARGE DOG.

CHARLES, PRINCE OF WALES, afterwards Charles II. aged 7. Born, 1630. Ascended the Throne, 1660. Died, 1685.

MARY, aged 6. Born, 1631. Afterwards Princess of Orange, and mother of William III.

JAMES, DUKE OF YORK, aged 4. Born, 1633. Ascended the throne as James II., 1685. Deposed, 1688. Died at St. Germain's, 1701.

ELIZABETH, aged 2. Born, 1635. Died unmarried at Carisbrook Castle.

ANNE, aged 1. Died in Infancy.

An old copy after Sir Anthony Van Dyck.

PLATE CXXXIV.

FRANCIS BACON, afterwards Baron Verulam and Viscount St. Alban's, Essayist, Statesman, Philosopher. Born at York House in the Strand, 1561, youngest son of Sir Nicholas Bacon, Keeper of the Great Seal to Queen Elizabeth. Entered Trinity College, Cambridge, in the twelfth year of his age. He visited Paris under the care of Sir Amias Paulet, Elizabeth's Minister at the French Court. On the death of his father, 1579, he returned to England. Admitted at Gray's Inn, 1575, and was sworn in Queen's Counsel Extraordinary, 1595. Sat as M.P. for the county of Middlesex, 1593. He was knighted, and under the reign of James, grew rapidly in fortune and favour. In 1604 he was appointed King's Counsel; Solicitor-General, 1607; Attorney-General, 1613; Keeper of the Great Seal, 1617; Lord Chancellor, 1618. Created Baron Verulam, 1618, and Viscount St. Alban's, 1621. Deprived of his high office, 1621, and withdrew from public life. Died at Highgate, 1626, and buried at St. Michael's, near St. Alban's. His essays were first published, 1597, and subsequently largely added to; "On the advancement of Learning," 1605; "Novum Organum," 1620.

"The founding of a new philosophy, the imparting of a new direction to the minds of speculators, this was the amusement of his leisure, the work of hours occasionally stolen from the Woolsack and the Council Board."

"The checkered spectacle of so much glory and so much shame."

Painted by Paul van Somer.

PLATE CXXXV.

WILLIAM CAMDEN, Antiquarian. Born in the Old Bailey, 1551. Educated at Christ's Hospital, St. Paul's School, and Oxford. Master at Westminster School, becoming headmaster, 1593.

Founded a professorship of History at Oxford. Died at Chislehurst, 1623, and was buried in Westminster Abbey. His most celebrated work is in Latin, entitled "Britannia," first published in 1586, giving a topographical description of Great Britain from the earliest times. He also wrote in Latin "Annals of Queen Elizabeth," 1615.

Painted in 1609 by Marc Gheeraedts.

PLATE CXXXVI.

SIR WALTER RALEIGH. Son of Walter Raleigh, of Fordel, Devonshire. Born at Hayes, near Budleigh-Salterton, 1552. Educated at Oriel College, Oxford. Sailed with Sir Humphrey Gilbert, 1578, to found a colony in North America. Held a captain's commission in Ireland against the rebels, 1580. Founded the American colony of Virginia and was knighted in 1584. Commanded the Queen's forces in Cornwall during the threatened Spanish invasion, 1587-88. Headed an expedition to Guiana, 1595. Held the post of Admiral in the attack on Cadiz, 1596. Imprisoned in the Tower by order of James I. on a charge of high treason, 1603, and during a period of thirteen years' incarceration, wrote his famous "History of the World." Beheaded in the Old Palace Yard, 1618, and buried in St. Margaret's, Westminster.

"Raleigh was a man of noble presence, of versatile and commanding genius, unquestionably one of the most splendid figures in a time unusually prolific of all splendid developments of humanity."

Painted probably by Federigo Zucharo, 1588.

PLATE CXXXVII.

WILLIAM SHAKSPEARE, Poet, Playwright, and Actor. Born at Stratford-on-Avon, 1564. Third child and first son of John and Mary (née Arden) Shakspeare, a glover and chamberlain of the borough. Went at the age of seven to the Grammar School and possibly began life as a boy actor, playing women's parts. In his eighteenth year he married Anne Hathaway, the daughter of a Shottery farmer. That some local trouble caused Shakspeare to leave home soon after his marriage seems likely, but little is known of the real cause of his coming to London or of his life there. Between 1585 and 1594 there is only one record concerning him. In 1597 he was able to return to Stratford and purchase the most important house, known as New Place. A mention of "Hamlet" being played occurs in 1589. The first printed play was "Henry VI., Part II.," in 1594; "Henry V." was produced in 1599. His works were first published collectively in one folio, 1623. In 1607 his eldest daughter, Susanna, was married to Mr. John Hall, and in the following year the poet was able to witness the baptism of his first granddaughter, at whose decease (then Lady Barnard) in 1670 his family was to become extinct. In 1612 Shakspeare bought property in London. The Globe Theatre, in which he was interested, was burned to the ground in 1613. He died on April 23rd, 1616, and was buried at Stratford-on-Avon.

"Judicio Pylium, Genio Socratem, arte Maronem,
Terra tegit, populus mæret, Olympus habet."

"With reverence look on his majestic face,
Proud to be less, but of his God-like race."

The picture, attributed to Richard Burbage, has in recent times been known as the Chandos Portrait. Dark, yellow-brown eyes; eyebrows broad and pale brown, with deeper touches of dark brown below them; moustache and beard yellow-brown; hair very dark sepia brown, and massive, concealing all but the lobe of the ear, which is pierced by a plain gold ring.

PLATE CXXXVIII.

THE GUNPOWDER PLOT CONSPIRATORS, viz., GUY FAWKES, ROBERT CATESBY, THOMAS PERCY, JOHN WRIGHT, CHRISTOPHER WRIGHT, ROBERT WINTER, THOMAS WINTER and THOMAS BATES.

GUY FAWKES, born in Yorkshire, 1570. Son of the Registrar of the Consistory Court of York Cathedral. Educated at the free school of that city. Served in the Spanish Army, under Archduke Albert, in Flanders. Selected by Catesby and Winter for carrying the plot into execution, but was taken red-handed, tried, and after having been put to the torture, was publicly executed in 1606.

ROBERT CATESBY, born, 1573, was the son of Sir William Catesby. Educated at Gloucester Hall, now Worcester College, Oxford. Joined the insurrection of the Earl of Essex, 1601. Originated the Gunpowder Plot, 1604. On the arrest of Fawkes he fled from London with the rest of the conspirators, but was overtaken and killed at Holbeach, in Staffordshire, 1605.

THOMAS PERCY, great grandson of Henry, fourth Earl of Northumberland. Born in 1560. Was converted to the Catholic faith early in life. Sent on a mission to King James, 1602, from whom he obtained promises of toleration for the English Catholics. These promises being unfulfilled, he joined the conspiracy, 1604. Killed with Catesby by the same shot, as they fought back to back.

JOHN and CHRISTOPHER WRIGHT, brothers-in-law of Percy. Converted to Catholicism, and took part in the insurrection of the Earl of Essex. Both were killed at Holbeach.

THOMAS WINTER, the first to join in the plot with Catesby. Served against the King of Spain in Flanders, and afterwards entered the service of Lord Monteagle. Executed with Guy Fawkes in Palace Yard, Westminster, 1606.

ROBERT WINTER, elder brother of Thomas Winter. Was at first strongly opposed to the plot, but eventually took an active part in it. Executed in St. Paul's Chuchyard, 1606.

THOMAS BATES, an old servant of Catesby. Beheaded with Robert Winter, 1606.

"The crime was too great, the meditated slaughter too remorseless, and the consequences of success in their plans too appalling, to permit any sentiment but horror; and even the merit they claimed as zealous and obedient sons of the only true Church was an addition to the hatefulness of their crime."

Engraved from the life by Crispin de Passe.

PLATE CXXXIX.

QUEEN ELIZABETH. Daughter of Henry VIII. and Anne Boleyn. Born at Greenwich, 1533. Committed to the Tower by her sister, Queen Mary, in 1554. Studied under Roger Ascham at her residence of Hatfield House, Hertfordshire. Ascended the throne in 1558. Restored the Protestant religion in England. Caused the execution of Mary, Queen of Scots, 1587. Assisted the French king, Henry of Navarre, and the Dutch Hugenots against the Catholics. In the thirtieth year of her reign occurred the destruction of the Spanish Armada by the English Fleet under Lord Howard of Effingham. Died at Richmond, 1603. Buried in Westminster Abbey.

"As a woman she was vain, fickle, fond of dress and of flattery; but as a queen, although cold-hearted and at times cruel, she was a great and patriotic sovereign."

Painted probably by Federigo Zucharo.

PLATE CXL.

WILLIAM CECIL, LORD BURGHLEY, K.G. Son of Richard Cecil, Master of the Robes to Henry VIII. Born at Bourn, Lincolnshire, 1520. Educated at Stamford and Grantham, and at St. John's College, Cambridge. Entered Gray's Inn, 1541.

Elected for Stamford, and appointed Master of Requests, 1547. Created Chief Secretary of State, 1558, and Master of the Court of Wards, 1561. Raised to the peerage ten years later, and elected Knight of the Garter and Lord High Treasurer, 1572. Died in London, 1598, and buried at Stamford.

"By him more than by any other single man during the last thirty years of his life was the history of England shaped. He was alike the originator and director of that policy, which, hitherto, has made Elizabeth's reign memorable above that of any other English sovereign."

Painted probably by Marc Gheeradts.

PLATE CXLI.

MARY, QUEEN OF SCOTS. Daughter of James V., King of Scotland, and Mary of Lorraine. Born at Linlithgow, 1542. Succeeded to the crown when scarcely a week old. Carried to France, 1548, and married in 1558 to the Dauphin, afterwards François II. Became Queen of France, 1559. On the death of her husband (1560) she returned to Scotland (1561). Married Darnley, 1565; and the Earl of Bothwell, 1567. Fled to England, 1568. Beheaded at Fotheringay Castle, 1587.

Painted by P. Oudry, in 1587.

PLATE CXLII.

SIR THOMAS GRESHAM, known as the "Merchant Royal." Son of Sir Richard Gresham, Lord Mayor of London. Born in London, 1519. Apprenticed to his uncle, Sir John Gresham, a wealthy London mercer, 1535. Educated at Gonville Hall (now Caius College), Cambridge. Admitted as a member of the Mercers' Company, 1543. Sent to Antwerp as King's factor, 1552. Knighted by Queen Elizabeth, 1559, and appointed English Ambassador to the Court of the Duchess of Parma, Regent of the Netherlands. Founded the Royal Exchange, 1566, and at his death left sufficient funds for the endowment of Gresham College. Died, 1579. Buried at St. Helen's, Bishopsgate.

"Gresham's character exhibits shrewdness, self-reliance, foresight, and tenacity of purpose, qualities, which coupled with great diligence and an innate love of commerce, account for his great success as merchant and financial agent."

Painted by Sir Antonio More.

PLATE CXLIII.

JOHN KNOX, the great apostle of the Scottish Reformation. Born at Gifford Gate, near Haddington, 1505. Educated at Haddington Grammar School and Glasgow University. Went to St. Andrew's, 1523, and openly proclaimed himself a Protestant in 1543. Sent as a prisoner to the French galleys, 1547, and liberated in 1549. Appointed Chaplain to Edward VI., and lived on terms of intimate intercourse with Cranmer and others of the English reformers. Retired to the Continent, 1553, and acted as pastor of a congregation at Geneva from 1556 to 1559. Recalled in 1559, and was the prime agent in the establishment of the Reformed Church in Scotland, 1560. Died at Edinburgh, 1572, and was buried at St. Giles' Church.

"Even if we should take exception to some things he did or encouraged, we may admire the consistent boldness, the deep earnestness, and the self-denying, unflinching zeal of the great Reformer."

Painter unknown—probably an Italian artist.

PLATE CXLIV.

HENRY, LORD DARNLEY. Son of Matthew Stuart, Earl of Lenox. Born in England, 1545. Married Mary, Queen of Scots, 1565, and was by her created Duke of Albany. Caused the assassination of David Rizzio in 1566, and was himself murdered at Kirk o' Field, near Edinburgh, 1567, and buried in the Chapel of Holyrood.

"He was handsome in appearance, accomplished in manners, but fatally destitute of all moral and intellectual power."

Sculptor unknown.

PLATE CXLV.

THOMAS CRANMER, D.D., First Protestant Archbishop of Canterbury. Born at Aslacton Manor, Nottinghamshire, 1489. Entered Jesus College, Cambridge, 1503. Took his degree of D.D. in 1523. Appointed Archdeacon of Taunton, 1528, and created Archbishop of Canterbury, 1532. Promoted the translation and circulation of the scriptures. Assisted also in the compilation of the Service-Book and the Articles of Religion. Committed to the Tower, 1553, whence he was removed with Ridley and Latimer to the Bocardo Prison, Oxford, 1554. In the hope of saving his life, he signed no fewer than six recantations, but was burnt at the stake opposite Balliol College, Oxford, 1556.

"His position was no doubt a difficult one; but his character was naturally pliable and timid, rather than resolute and consistent. His courage returned at the end, however, and he died protesting his repentance for his unworthy weakness in changing his faith, and showing an unexpected fortitude in the midst of the flames."

Painted by G. Flicius, 1546.

PLATE CXLVI.

HUGH LATIMER, D.D., Bishop of Worcester, one of the most distinguished of the English Reformers. Born at Thurcaston, Leicestershire, 1485. Educated at Cambridge. Created Bishop of Worcester, 1535. Committed to the Tower after the fall of Cromwell, Earl of Essex, in 1540, and not released until 1547. Imprisoned again by Queen Mary, and removed with Ridley and Cranmer to Oxford, 1554, where he suffered martyrdom at the stake opposite Balliol College, 1555.

"He was brave, honest, devoted and energetic, homely and popular, yet free from all violence; a martyr and a hero, yet a plain, simple-hearted and unpretending man."

Painted by an unknown artist, 1555.

PLATE CXLVII.

LADY JANE GREY. Daughter of Henry Grey, Marquess of Dorset, afterwards Duke of Suffolk; and great-granddaughter of Henry VII. Born at Bradgate, Leicestershire, 1537. Educated by Aylmer, afterwards Bishop of London. Married to Lord Guildford Dudley, 1553, whose father, the Duke of Northumberland, persuaded King Edward VI. to nominate Lady Jane as his successor to the throne. Persuaded by her parents to assume the title of Queen, 1553, but after a reign of ten days, fell before the power of Mary, the king's sister. Beheaded with her husband in the Tower, 1554; buried in the Church of St. Peter ad Vincula, within the Tower.

"All the beauty, learning and innocence, which bestow so much interest on the person and fortunes of Lady Jane Grey, were of no avail; she, who had never sighed for a crown, but protested against the efforts made in her favour, was considered a usurper, and shared in the obloquy of her father-in-law."

Painted by Lucas de Heere.

PLATE CXLVIII.

HENRY VIII. Second son of Henry VII. Born at Greenwich, 1491. Ascended the throne, 1509. Married Catherine of Arragon, 1509; Anne Boleyn, 1533; Jane Seymour, 1536; Anne of Cleves, 1540; Catherine Howard, 1540; and Catherine Parr, 1543. Published a book against Luther, in defence of the seven sacraments, which gained him the title of " Fidei Defensor." Declared himself Head of the Church, 1532. Confiscated a large quantity of church property and caused many of the larger monasteries to be destroyed. Died at Westminster, 1547, and buried at Windsor.

"The ruin of English freedom, which had been industriously begun by the cunning and perseverance of his father, was completed by his brutal determination and insane love of power. No pity nor remorse, no respect for man or tenderness for woman stood in the way of his selfish gratification."

Painted from a portrait by Luke Hornebolt, in 1554.

PLATE CXLIX.

ANNE BOLEYN. Second Queen of Henry VIII. and mother of Queen Elizabeth. Was the daughter of Sir Thomas Boleyn, afterwards Earl of Wiltshire and Ormond. Born at Blickling, in Norfolk, 1507. Sent to the French Court, 1519, and became Maid of Honour to Queen Catherine, 1527. Married Henry VIII., 1533, but losing his favour, was committed to the Tower on a charge of infidelity to her husband, and beheaded, 1536.

"There is much room to doubt that she was guilty of the heinous offences laid to her charge, but although she met her end with singular cheerfulness and courage, her conduct in the time of her prosperity had been so arrogant and overbearing, that few men in those days pitied her fate, or doubted that it had been righteously decreed."

Painter unknown.

PLATE CL.

CATHERINE OF ARRAGON. First Queen of Henry VIII. and mother of Queen Mary. Daughter of Ferdinand and Isabella of Spain. Born at Alcalá de Henares, 1485. Married to Arthur, Prince of Wales, 1501, and to his brother, Henry VIII., 1509. Her divorce, in 1533, was the occasion of Henry's open defiance of the Pope, and led to the complete separation of the English Church from Rome. Retired to Ampthill, Bedfordshire, in 1533, and afterwards to Kimbolton Castle, Huntingdonshire. Died at Kimbolton, 1536. Buried at Peterborough.

"Her personal character was unimpeachable, and her disposition sweet and gentle; she occupies a prominent position in English history, not so much for what she herself was, but rather for what she was the occasion of—The Reformation."

Painter unknown.

PLATE CLI.

THOMAS WOLSEY, Cardinal. Born at Ipswich, 1471, and said to have been the son of a butcher of that town. Educated at Magdalen College, Oxford. Took his degree at the age of fifteen. Became Rector of Lymington, Somersetshire, 1500. Appointed Dean of Lincoln, 1508. Created Bishop of Lincoln and Archbishop of York, 1514, and became Prime Minister and Lord High Chancellor, 1515. Promoted by the Pope to the dignity of Cardinal in the same year. Resided in great magnificence at Whitehall. Built Hampton Court Palace, which he afterwards presented to Henry VIII., and founded Christ Church, Oxford. Incurred the king's displeasure, and was driven from the Court, 1529. Arrested for high treason, 1530, and died at Leicester on his way to London for trial.

"Haughty and insolent to his enemies and those whose claims ran counter to his own, to his dependants and inferiors he was generous, affable and humane. He was plainly a man of large and splendid capacity, and he seems on the whole to have been a faithful, diligent, conscientious, and salutory counsellor and servant of the monarch who so long and entirely trusted to him."

Painter unknown.

PLATE CLII.

KING HENRY V., the hero of Agincourt. Born at Monmouth, 1387. Eldest son of Henry of Bolingbroke, afterwards Henry IV., and Mary de Bohun. Succeeded his father, 1413. Married Katherine of Valois, by whom he was recognised as successor to the throne of France, to the exclusion of the Dauphin. The success of his arms in France, from 1415 to 1419 are amongst the most brilliant in the annals of this country. He died near Paris, 1422.

Painter unknown.

PLATE CLIII.

GEOFFREY CHAUCER, Poet. Born somewhere near the year 1340, his family being apparently citizens of London. The accounts of his earlier years and education are vague and unsatisfactory; but he was certainly a man of extensive learning, and had a liberal education. He is generally believed to have been bred to the law. He was with the army of Edward III. in 1359, when it invaded France, and was taken prisoner. He was one of the valets of the King's Chamber, 1367. Married about this time Philippa, eldest daughter of Sir Payne Roet, and sister of Lady Katherine Swynford, who married John of Gaunt, who was Chaucer's chief patron. Went on the King's service to Genoa and Florence, 1372-3. Was appointed Comptroller of the Customs, 1374. Appointed Clerk to the King's Works, 1389, but was dismissed, 1391. He was at length restored to favour, 1399, but died, probably at his house in Westminster, on the 25th October, 1400, and buried in Westminster Abbey. His "Canterbury Tales" were the compilation of Chaucer's later years.

"Dan Chaucer, well of English undefyled."

Painted on a square piece of oak panel. Painter unknown.

PLATE CLIV.

EDWARD, THE BLACK PRINCE, Prince of Wales. Eldest son of Edward III. Born at Woodstock, 1330. Invested with the Earldom and County of Chester, 1333, and created Duke of Cornwall, 1337. Educated by Dr. Walter Burley, of Merton College, Oxford. Knighted by his father at La Hague, and won the Battle of Crécy, 1346. In this action fell John, King of Bohemia, whose crest and motto—three ostrich feathers with the words "Ich dien"—the Black Prince adopted, and they have ever since been borne by the Prince of Wales. Present at the siege of Calais, 1347, and utterly routed the French at Poitiers, 1356. Undertook an expedition into Spain, where in behalf of Peter the Cruel, he gained the battle of Navarette, 1367. Died at Westminster, 1376, and was buried in Canterbury Cathedral.

"It may be said that Edward's reign witnessed the culmination of chivalry, and in the Black Prince, the truest knight and bravest prince in Christendom, possessed a splendid example of its virtues and vices."

Sculptor unknown.

www.ingramcontent.com/pod-product-compliance
Lightning Source LLC
Chambersburg PA
CBHW020233240426

43672CB00006B/508